MW01658512

To Paul,

Continued Success.

MARKETING FINANCIAL SERVICES TO $ENIORS

A Program for Tapping the Most Affluent Market in America Today

Financial Professionals Endorse the Concepts in

Marketing Financial Services to Seniors . . .

"I want to take a moment and thank you for all the very valuable information you have assembled and made available to advisors who serve the senior market. The value of such information is twofold: 1) ***You provide information that is exceptionally important for those who are serving seniors by defining solutions that are most suitable.*** *The end result is the advisor is more knowledgeable on how to conduct good, 'clean' business in meeting the needs of a senior. And 2) you provide an excellent 'marketing system' that relatively few are doing, hence giving us a competitive advantage."*

M. Sears, President
Sears Retirement Planning Services, Inc.

◆

"Seminars are going great! I have done one a month ever since I started with the system, and ***my life has been completely turned around.*** *I can't thank you enough!"*

M. Spedding
Investors Capital

◆

"Just one month into marketing your annuity system, and ***the results are incredible.*** *I have an open case inventory of thirty-two contacts with what I consider to be excellent sales possibilities."*

P. Matienzo, CLU, ChFC, LUTCF
President, M.D. Financial and Insurance, Inc.

◆

"I'm an independent CFP and Certified Senior Advisor just getting into the senior market. I am selling some LTC plans, and ***these prospects are starting to open doors for annuity and life insurance sales*** *. . . I think if I continue to follow the path that, thanks to you, I am going down, even as an individual without an office, I can make a very good living and have plenty of time for my family."*

R. Scott, CFP, CSA
Locust Street Securities

"Greetings from south Florida! I just want to express my satisfaction regarding your fine annuity marketing system. Even though our marketing system is in its infancy, ***the initial results have been stunning.****"*

B. Miller, Vice President
Alliance Financial Group

◆

" . . . I was a bit apprehensive when I first ordered your system; however, after a short period of time my thinking has changed . . . I must say the results are nothing short of phenomenal . . . I truly have more qualified prospects than I have time to see. ***I only wish I had seen this five years ago.****"*

D. Adams, Certified Annuity Counselor and
Certified Elder Planning Specialist
Senior Financial Services

◆

"Since I've started using seminars and Larry Klein's newsletter, as well as employing many of his other systems in my practice, ***my production has skyrocketed! I don't work evenings or weekends.*** *Thanks in large part to Larry Klein and his systems, my employees, family, and my church have enjoyed success beyond my expectations."*

S. Hansen
Senior First, Inc.

◆

"I have used just about every marketing scheme known to man, but ***I have to take my hat off to you when it comes to your annuity marketing program.*** *. . . The only problem I have now is that my wife sees what is going on in my business and has demanded to move to a larger, more expensive house!"*

N. Frankle, CFP
Frankle & Associates

◆

"Again, overall we're very pleased with your systems. We highly recommend them to anyone who is looking to increase business. ***We feel that they were the easiest to use of anything we'd ever implemented before.*** *The instruction manuals were turnkey. We could always read them within an hour or two and be implementing them the next day. We're really pleased with everything."*

R. Caruthers, CFS, Senior Financial Advisor
The Tax and Investment Advisory

"As you know from marketing your own services, people do not beat a path to your door just because you have a great idea. We have tried seminars with mediocre results. That all changed when we met Larry Klein: He is a master marketer. He showed us how to market our plan to a lot more agents and their clients . . . ***you will never have a shortage of qualified prospects.*** *Your only decision will be how many hours you want to work, and how many new clients you wish to add to your practice."*

E. LICHTIG, PRESIDENT
GSL ADVISORY

◆

"You've got a true-blue believer here. *Please understand I have been on the edge of quitting—I've been surviving, but not thriving—now I see the opportunity to transfuse my practice with much needed 'new blood' and can do it in a manner I love."*

F. BIRNEL
AMERICAN EXPRESS FINANCIAL ADVISORS

◆

"I want to let you know how instrumental your seminar program has been in helping me take my business to the next level. . . . ***Our biggest problem is getting back to all the people who request appointments."***

J. D. FRANKLIN, FINANCIAL CONSULTANT
J. J. B. HILLIARD, W. L. LYONS, INC.

◆

"To use an analogy from baseball, you hit the ball out of the park with this program. ***Larry, we were stunned when calls started coming in from people with modest annuities but large portfolio holdings—some multi-millions!*** *We had no idea that we would be reaching an affluent market of investors with significant interest in portfolio management."*

M. MUELLER, SENIOR FINANCIAL ADVISOR
SENIOR RETIREMENT RESOURCES

◆

"Larry, thanks again for your time and advice. ***I wish you had been my manager fifteen years ago when I entered the business.*** *I would be much more successful than I am now."*

D. OVERSON
FFP SECURITIES

Marketing Financial Services to $eniors

A Program for Tapping the Most Affluent Market in America Today

Larry Klein • CPA • MBA
Certified Senior Advisor
Registered Investment Advisor

NF Communications, Inc.
Walnut Creek, California

NF COMMUNICATIONS, INC.
1700 North Broadway, Suite 405
Walnut Creek, CA 94596

Third edition 2004
Designed and typeset by Robert Mott & Associates • Keswick, Virginia
Edited by Just Write • Keswick, Virginia
Printed in the United States of America

ISBN: 0-9662062-6-6

Other Books by Larry Klein:

400 Greatest Financial Jokes

Annuity Owner Mistakes

Asset Protection and Wealth Preservation

Beat the Dow—Invest like Warren Buffet

How to Avoid Mistakes in Buying Long-Term Care

Retirement Investing

Mistakes Retirees Make With Their Finances

CONTENTS

INTRODUCTION

The financial press is having a love affair with baby boomers.

Writers are enamored with how much these forty- and fifty-somethings will inherit and how much business this will create for the financial services industry. Trade publications spout advice to investment professionals about how to capture the transfer of $10 trillion of wealth. It will be a rosy day ahead, they promise.

But why wait around anticipating tomorrow when the baby boomers' *parents* have the wealth today? Why wait for the chicks to hatch when the roosters and hens already have the golden eggs? The senior market possesses incredible investment wealth right now! Seniors have unmet financial and communication needs, and the business opportunities they present today are staggering.

This book is about tapping that wealth right now by helping today's seniors—and profiting handsomely. Few financial firms or professionals understand this market. Banks, securities firms, and insurance companies are steeped in a product-focused mentality. They have done a poor job of developing a customer-oriented focus, especially with seniors.

Common Misconceptions about Seniors

- "Old folks" take too long to make a decision.
- They won't do anything; their money is already settled.
- They just want bonds—how can a stockbroker make any money from them?
- They're too conservative.

Be thankful your competitors believe these fallacies, as it opens a window of opportunity for you to prosper in the senior market. Let your competitors be happy with $50,000 checks from their baby-boomer clients while you prospect the senior market and get $500,000 checks.

◆

> *Focusing on the senior market has been profitable and enjoyable. It is great to assist older couples or widows/widowers to make sure they have the peace of mind knowing all avenues and options have been looked over. [I get] personal and professional satisfaction.*
>
> **DON ROSS,** CERTIFIED SENIOR ADVISOR
> AMERICAN EXPRESS FINANCIAL ADVISORS

◆

Selling and providing value are synonymous. However, that does not mean you can simply tell your story in any old way and get the business. There are issues to understand about how seniors make their decisions. There are methods of presenting your services that will make you more effective when communicating with seniors. I cover these issues and methods in this book.

Being successful in the financial services business is mostly about marketing strategies and sales presentations, positioning, and tactical issues for penetrating a selected market. A method exists for being a very effective, profitable marketer and salesperson: a method that is totally consistent with serving people well with dignity and acting in their best interests. That's what this book is about: helping seniors to improve their financial circumstances.

This book is based on a program already in practice. It has helped thousands of average professionals become big producers by focusing on the most affluent individuals and taking a strategic, step-by-step approach for penetrating their share of this huge market. Seniors control the bulk of the investable assets in the United States in the new century. Get ready to explode your business by working effectively with seniors.

1 Who Is a Senior?

Every article or book you read will define seniors differently.

Some use an age distinction, starting the cutoff at fifty or fifty-five. Yet it's ludicrous to define people in their fifties as seniors or even part of the "mature" market. Most are working, still years away from retirement, with kids in college and weddings to finance; many are even students themselves. Their primary concerns are their children, paying bills, and saving for retirement. In my experience, today's fifty-five-year-old has little in common with the average seventy-year-old. The fifty-five-year-old of today is more of a "mature thirty-year-old." Therefore, in this book, we are not interested in the group who are baby boomers and in no way can be considered seniors.

In *Marketing Financial Services to Seniors,* we are more interested in this kind of senior: likely to be retired, has health concerns, is living alone or with a spouse, has financed all major purchases, and is likely to be debt-free. He or she wants to enjoy life, maintain financial security, and minimize hassles.

Studies of the senior market have done a fairly sophisticated job of segmenting it. It's worthwhile to spend a little time learning about these subsegments, as detailed information on the mature market and its constituent parts will give you insights into marketing and sales approaches that can pay handsome dividends. In addition to what you learn from this book, you may want to read some of the referenced studies.

In 1994, Geoffery Meredith and Charles Schewe used the "cohort" concept to assess the members of the senior market.[1] They divided seniors into six distinct groups ("cohorts") that were defined by events that occurred at a critical point in the seniors' lives.

For example, the Depression Cohorts are people born 1912 to 1921 (ages seventy-nine to eighty-eight in the year 2000). Much of the way this group behaves and makes decisions, particularly about money, is defined by its experiences during the depression years. Given their early experience of financial catastrophe, members of this group are, as you might expect, compulsive savers. (For example, my wife's grandmother saved pieces of string and cloth for potential reuse until her death.) Creative marketers developed the S&P 500 linked CD for this group as a chance for conservative investors to participate in stock market gains while having the comfort of an FDIC-insured CD at all times.

This group is also likely to tell you they cannot afford long-term care insurance. Yet, while reviewing a couple of Depression Cohorts' investments, you might notice they have an annuity generating $20,000 of annual deferred income that they never touch. They think of this annuity money as part of their financial cushion and never even consider it a financial resource unless an emergency occurs. This group will indeed make financial changes as long as you respect their need for plenty of financial security.

Two other senior groups and their distinctive characteristics:

- **THE WORLD WAR II COHORTS.** Born 1922 to 1927 and aged seventy-three to seventy-eight in 2000, members of this group have a strong tendency toward deferred gratification. Appeal to them by preserving and continuing to build wealth. These are the best cohorts for estate planning services. As a group, they are also ideal for money management services. Do not assume they want to

[1] Geoffery Meredith and Charles Schewe. "The Power of Cohorts," *American Demographics.* December 1994. *www.demographics.com/publications/ad/94_ad09412_ad/ad734.htm.*

keep their money in bonds just because they are in their seventies. Many members of this group are as interested in the next hot stock as you are, because they like to see their wealth grow.

- **THE POST-WAR COHORTS.** As children of post-war economic expansion, the Post-War Cohorts enjoy feeling comfortable, secure, and familiar. This group, born 1928 to 1945 and aged fifty-five to seventy-two in 2000, enjoys spending money on travel, homes, and entertainment. They also think they know more than they do regarding financial matters. While some are indeed financially astute, many members of this group are do-it-yourselfers and often don't know what they need to when going it alone. You'll need to educate and point out errors to earn the business of some of this group.

Another social scientist, George P. Moschis of the Center for Mature Consumer Studies at the University of Georgia, uses a psychological segmentation that will help most salespeople understand their senior markets even better. He categorizes seniors not by age, but by four behavioral types: [2]

MOSCHIS' PSYCHOLOGICAL SEGMENTS

- **HEALTHY INDULGERS,** who feel accomplished and are typically financially comfortable and take life by the reins;
- **FRAIL RECLUSES,** who stay inside because of their failing health;
- **HEALTHY HERMITS,** who are physically sound but maintain a solitary existence or stay at home alone or with a spouse; and
- **AILING OUTGOERS,** who have health limitations but don't let this stop them from getting out.

[2] George P. Moschis. *Gerontographics: Life Stage Segmentation for Marketing Strategy Development* [Westport, CT: Greenwood Publishing Group, Inc. (Quorum), 1996].

While they are informative, such models have marketing limitations for the financial advisor. While Moschis' work is interesting and possibly useful for the marketing team back at the home office, it's too detailed to be workable for the individual producer wanting to do more business in the senior market. Likewise, when authors Carol Morgan and Doran Levy segment seniors by attitudes (into categories such as "proactive," "faithful," "patient," "optimistic," and "disillusioned"[3]), I'm unmoved. I have not yet found where to buy a mailing list of seniors who are optimists, so I do not consider this segmentation useful for the financial services practitioner.

Successful marketing in financial services requires a volume approach where the same products or services can be sold to a large base of prospects. There is neither time in the professional's day nor money in the marketing budget to serve multiple subsegments of any target market. It's important, however, to understand these subsegments so that, when you're giving a sales presentation, you have some insight into your prospect's characteristics. Such insights could help the financial producer recommend the right product or service, present the recommendation in the most palatable manner, make a sale, and help the client.

Most marketing studies do not present simple models that the producer can use to increase sales. Although intellectually interesting, there's not much the insurance agent or stockbroker can do with these distinctions for marketing. So I will present a simple model that I developed through my experience and the observations of others.

First, as already stated, I am defining a senior as someone who is already retired or very close to retirement. These people begin to have serious concerns about health, finances, and mortality. They take on a realistic view of what's important that the working person, even five years younger, does not exhibit. This older group shifts from a worldview of "I'll be around a while," to one of "This is the last third of the race—I'd better make the best of it."

As far as I can observe, crossing the precipice of retirement is a

[3] Carol Morgan and Doran Levy. *Segmenting the Mature Market* (Chicago, IL: Irwin Professional Publishing Company, 1993).

fundamental, life-altering event, when new values take center stage. People who are retired or close to it are typically sixty to sixty-five years old.[4] In 1993, labor statistics indicated that at age fifty-five, only 38 percent of men in the United States were still in the labor force, and by age sixty-five, only 16 percent of men were still working.[5] For simplicity, we will use age sixty-plus to define a senior and consider that most workers have retired or will soon be retired by age sixty. In fact, there is some statistical support for this life demarcation at age sixty as noted by *American Demographics* magazine:

> *More than half (54 percent) of the population aged fifty and older is under age sixty-five. By all of the measures we studied, the differences between the two youngest age groups, those aged fifty to fifty-four and those aged fifty-five to fifty-nine, were relatively small. But by age sixty, change became more noticeable. For example, the percentage of people who are widowed jumps from 7 percent of the fifty-five- to fifty-nine-year-olds to 13 percent among sixty- to sixty-four-year-olds.*[6]

By segmenting the market by age, it becomes much easier for the financial services professional to identify and target this market. It's easy to buy mailing lists of people of a certain age, and many states make public their motor vehicle records, which identify people by age.

I have purposefully simplified the definition of seniors so that you have one that works for you. As financial planners, we need a way to easily define our market. When I send seminar invitations, I send them to a list of people aged sixty to seventy-nine, in the middle and upper-middle income Zip codes in my area, to households with incomes of $50,000 and above. This produces attendees who have investable net worths exceeding

---

[4] For the population over fifty, the median retirement age is sixty-one, and by age sixty-six, 71 percent are retired, according to Morgan and Levy in *Segmenting the Mature Market* (see prior footnote).

[5] "Sixty-Five Plus in the United States." U.S. Census Bureau, 1995.

[6] Louis G. Pol, Michael G. May, and Frank R. Hartranft. "Eight Stages of Aging," *American Demographics*. August 1992.

$250,000. The invitation plainly states, "For Investors Aged Sixty and Over."

Indeed, there may be some fifty-eight-year-olds who would be good prospects and some eighty-four-year-olds who could benefit from our working together. However, I have noticed that when I go out of the boundaries delineated above, my success rate for finding prospects who are homogeneous falls off considerably. Prospecting outside these boundaries produces individuals who have either a baby-boomer mentality (for the lower ages) or significant health issues (for the upper ages) that limit their motivation to make any changes.

From Census Bureau estimates of people age fifty-five and older and sixty-five and older, I extrapolate that the market of people aged sixty-plus is forty-four million—about 17 percent of the U.S. population. These forty-four million people are the focus of this book, with particular emphasis on those in the upper half ranked by accumulated net worth.

If you focus on this half of senior households, about twenty-two million people, you will have all the business you will ever need.

Chapter 1 Summary

Although there are many ways to define and segment the senior market, this book sticks to a definition that will help you target the most affluent. Here, the most desirable senior client is someone who already

- is aged sixty-plus,
- is retired or close to retirement,
- may have health concerns, and
- takes financial issues seriously.

2 Why Sell to Seniors?

The senior market has some of the greatest unmet financial needs.

Seniors in retirement are seldom addressed and regularly overlooked as valuable customers.

Consider This . . .

1. How much material is produced by insurance companies and securities firms about saving for retirement? But how much have you read about strategies for investing *during* retirement?
2. How often have you read that people do not save enough for retirement? How much do you hear about those who are retired and *have* saved enough?
3. How many strategies are publicized for investing your 401(k) money? How often do you learn new strategies for *harvesting* 401(k) money?
4. How much press does dollar cost averaging (a popular technique for accumulating) get versus systematic *withdrawals* (a technique used by seniors for harvesting)?
5. How hot a news item are dot-com and Internet stocks when compared to *dividend-paying* stocks?

The entire financial system is biased toward accumulation rather than preservation or harvesting, which are the concerns of seniors. Then why sell to seniors? Because you have expertise, products, and services seniors need—and there are forty-four million people who need your help.

What's more, there are at least seven other solid business reasons to serve seniors.

Reason #1: Seniors Have More Money

The best advice I ever heard about marketing was this: *If you want to have a successful restaurant, locate it where there are hungry people.* You're in the money business, so which group do you want to prospect? What better market than people who are hungry and have money to spend? For the financial service professional, that's the senior market.

MEDIAN VALUE OF SELECTED ASSETS BY AGE OF HOUSEHOLDER

	Motor Vehicles	Interest-Earning Financial Accounts	Home	IRA/Keogh	Stocks/Mutual Fund Shares
Median Value	$5,249	$3,607	$43,078	$11,638	$5,469
Younger than 35	$4,138	$1,273	$15,283	$4,411	$2,074
35 to 44	$5,466	$2,325	$31,082	$8,634	$4,563
45 to 54	$6,634	$3,717	$45,869	$11,993	$5,160
55 to 64	$6,352	$6,587	$59,128	$18,023	$9,077
65 and older	$4,753	$15,337	$63,284	$15,136	$19,938

Source: Census Bureau, Survey of Income and Program Participation

Financial professionals often ignore what they first learned in Finance 101: the power of compounding. Compounding depends upon two variables: the rate earned on money and the length of time the money has been at work. So if you want to meet people with large net worths, either focus on the handful of people who founded high technology companies (and earned a very high return on their money); or focus on the easy-to-find, forty-four million people who have been alive for six decades or more (and time has compounded their nest eggs).

◆

I decided to work with seniors because they control a lot of money and need the security I can provide. Seminars and the newsletter seem to work the best, and I have doubled my income by using them.

GARY BAGLEY, FINANCIAL ADVISOR

◆

Reason #2: Seniors Are Concerned about Their Money

Seniors have more time to focus on their money than anyone else. After all, if you don't need to go to work every day, you have a lot more time to think about and take action on personal matters that are important to you—health, leisure, sports, and your money.

Most working people simply have no time and have not placed a priority on their investments. Between working long hours, caring for children, possibly caring for aging parents, and trying to give something back to the community with volunteer work, they have little energy left to take care of their money. In addition, working people do not yet feel the risk of losing a salary. Reality to a forty-year-old is the receipt of a paycheck every two weeks. They believe this will continue for another twenty to twenty-five years, creating some psychological comfort about their financial situation. And when people are comfortable, they have little motivation to act.

From a marketing viewpoint, it hardly makes sense to prospect forty-year-old investors. They have not achieved their peak earnings, and they are about to reach their peak spending (e.g., children attending college or getting married). If they have savings, the major portion is tied up in their 401(k) plans where you can't get at it. If you want to serve this market for altruistic reasons to help them better prepare for retirement, that's a noble endeavor. However, you will need to have far more clients and work harder than if you had fewer senior clients with significant net worths.

Reason #3: Seniors Have Control of Their Money

Seniors, who are usually retired, have control of their funds. Their 401(k) or other qualified retirement funds have been rolled over to a self-directed IRA. They have already sent their kids to college and paid for the weddings. Odds are, the house is paid off and they are net savers. They have funds in their control to invest.

In fact, after extensive analysis of the U.S. Bureau of Labor Statistics Consumer Expenditure Survey data from 1960 to 1986, researchers at the University of Pennsylvania concluded that the elderly tend to save more than they spend. On a per capita basis, people aged sixty-five and older saved more than younger people do. Thus, even during late life, a substantial number of older Americans save a large portion of their available income.[7]

And to restate the most important factor from the standpoint of prospecting efficiency, seniors have been alive longer, which means they have higher net worths[8]. This market segment (age fifty-five-plus) has more discretionary income to spend than any other. In the U.S. alone, senior citizens account for almost three-quarters of the nation's assets and almost half of the discretionary spending power. Among heads of household aged fifity-five and older, 75 percent own their own homes, and 83 percent of those homes are mortgage-free. The spending power of people over age fifty is five times greater than that of people under age thirty.

---

[7] George P. Moschis. *Marketing Strategies for the Mature Market* [Westport, CT: Greenwood Publishing Group, Inc. (Quorum), 1994].

[8] *The Golden Opportunity* (Hartford, CT: LIMRA, 1996).

Reason #4: Seniors Are an Easy Group to Prospect

It's easy to find these forty-four million people. In fact, as you would expect, most of these seniors do not work outside the home.[9] This makes them easy to locate, visit, and call during daytime hours. Compare this to prospecting people who are busy with jobs, kids, and finding a few hours to relax.

◆

When I first got into financial planning, I did not have a real desire to work with any specific group of people. I spent the first six months trying anything to make income. I used a "shotgun" approach and tried to hit anything that was out there. In the fall of '87, I was fortunate enough to book two seminars with a local lifecare community. My presentations were no doubt crude and probably boring, but people came and I wrote business from it. From that point, I decided to make seniors my niche, using the rationale that, if I am going to be chasing people for business, I may as well chase people who have money and will see me during the day.

I have focused on seniors for the last thirteen years. I have found that by focusing on this group, I do not have to spend a lot of time learning about other issues. Instead, I am able to direct my energies to learning how seniors think and make decisions. Every day I am getting better at seeing the world through my clients' eyes.

ALLEN PERRY, SENIOR ADVISOR

◆

Reason #5: Seniors Are Motivated

Imagine that you had no paycheck and no future possibility of one. Might you pay a lot more attention to your money—how much it's earning, where you spend it, how much you spend, how to invest it, etc.? For most seniors, health and money are their primary concerns. And that's good for you.

[9] Moschis, *Gerontographics.*

◆

Seniors are not as concerned with returns and are more security oriented than their younger peers. They have the money, and they are concerned with keeping it.

STEVEN SAMO, FINANCIAL ADVISOR

◆

Seniors are more likely to attend seminars, respond to direct mail, bring urgency to their decisions, and take financial decisions more seriously. Would you rather work with people who fear making a mistake and want good advice, or the forty-year-old who thinks every financial answer can be found in *Money* magazine and on the Internet?

You may be thinking, *But seniors are difficult to close.* Let me address that thought before we move forward.

It's true that seniors are difficult to sell if you've been selling to baby boomers and then have a meeting with a senior. You may simply be unaccustomed to the way information needs to be conveyed to seniors and what they find important. Your presentation needs to be very different. In my experience, seniors will buy based on trust, not on the merits of the plan or investment, or the logical reason to proceed. They will look first to trust you and then proceed in their decision.

Heed this: If you do not spend adequate time in selling yourself before your services or products, forget it. Even if you offered the senior a guaranteed investment, it won't sell until you create the critical trust component.

Compare how a senior invests (based on trust) to the forty-year-old. The younger investor maintains a stock portfolio with an online broker, makes changes in 401(k) allocations via a telephone or computer, uses the ATM machine, has been inside the bank only once, and does not know the name of anyone who works at his or her bank branch. Personal trust is not an element in these financial decisions.

Many seniors, however, enjoy going into the bank. They develop a relationship with the personnel. Many wise banks have set out coffee and donuts each morning along with a stack of newspapers. I have had some seniors attend my seminars two to three times before making an appointment to see me—even though I presented the same material at each seminar! But these people needed the extra exposure to feel comfortable with me. Bottom line: Pay attention to the high-touch component of the relationship.

Before making a judgment about the difficulty of selling to seniors, consider that you may not yet have the proper approach to tap this market. Fortunately, you can learn the proper approach in this book.

Reason #6: Seniors Offer Multiple Opportunities for Income

Selling multiple services to seniors is indeed possible. In a study by Moschis, 66 percent of respondents answered "strongly/somewhat agree" to the statement, "I would rather buy several services (like financial and insurance) from one place than deal with a different company for each service."[10]

◆

By focusing on seniors, we have been able to help address many problems at once, and have been able to help our clients attain financial freedom.

MAHALO NUI LOA, FINANCIAL ADVISOR

◆

INCOME OPPORTUNITIES WITH SENIORS

- **FEE-BASED INVESTMENT MANAGEMENT.** Many seniors lose the inclination as they age to watch a portfolio day to day. They willingly pay someone on a fee basis to do the job. Investment management is a great way to generate an annual income from your clients.
- **HEALTH INSURANCE.** As this is being written, there is a movement away from HMOs, which have earned a bad reputation in the press. Seniors are starting to turn back toward traditional Medigap

[10] Moschis, *Gerontographics.*

insurance, and this creates an opportunity for health insurance sales with annual residuals.

- **ESTATE PLANNING.** Providing the opportunity for hourly fees for consultation or insurance sales, estate planning also carries large premiums. In fact, in 1994, seniors over age sixty-five purchased only 3 percent of life policies issued, but paid 12 percent of the premiums collected. Large premiums equal large commissions.[11]
- **LONG-TERM CARE INSURANCE.** It's the only part of the life and health market experiencing double-digit growth. While 10 percent of the senior population now owns a policy, this figure could jump to well over 50 percent to include everyone who can afford some coverage. Again, it's an opportunity for annual residuals for the producer. In fact, policies that offer long-term care at home should be a "lay-up" sale for the insurance professional. A *USA Today* study showed that seniors ranked "a move into a nursing home" as their number one fear.[12] With that kind of motivator, sales of home care policies should be simple.
- **ANNUITIES.** There are billions of annuity dollars already in the hands of seniors.[13] However, most have older, non-competitive rates and structures. You can help seniors exchange this to better annuities (when appropriate) or in the case where the annuity will be left to heirs, convert to life policies. This is an excellent commission-generating strategy. Additionally, immediate annuities, which have not been popular in recent years, may become more popular as seniors live longer and seek out another source of income.
- **REVERSE MORTGAGES.** Although this product is still in its infancy, financial professionals are in the perfect position to unlock this home equity for seniors' benefit. I contend that this product's

---

[11] Morgan and Levy, *Segmenting the Mature Market.*

[12] Moschis, *Gerontographics.*

[13] Forty-six percent of annuities are owned by people in households with someone aged sixty-plus. Source: Equifax Financial Forum.

lack of success has been due to poor distribution and poor communication. These mortgages are sold through mortgage brokers who typically sell to people in their thirties, forties, and fifties. They have had little experience selling a mortgage to a seventy-year-old and, by all statistics, are failing at it. Result: Even though the first reverse mortgage loan was made in 1961, by 1999, only fifty-five thousand commercial reverse mortgages had been granted to homeowners.[14] This industry has simply failed to train its selected sales force in having an effective conversation with a senior.

Reason #7: Doing Business with Seniors Is Easy

My friends who are prospecting baby boomers tell me how the low brokerage fees on the Internet are cutting into their business and how clients are demanding discounted commissions. The average baby boomer (a member of what I call the "skeptical generation") wants everything proven: "Why should I do business with you when I can read *Money* magazine or log onto *cnnfn.com* and find out which funds to buy?"

◆

Focusing solely on seniors has increased my business by approximately 80 percent. Before using your systems, I would generate approximately ten qualified, interested prospects per month. Now, it averages about fifty per month. I feel that I am more effective with seniors than with other groups primarily because, as a group, seniors seem to be more respectful of advice given from a professional. They don't have the "know it all" attitude that other groups can have.

KEVIN W. STOCKTON, CFP, RIA
LEGACY FINANCIAL

◆

[14] National Center for Home Equity Conversion, *http://www.reverse.org/info.data.htm,* 11/3/99.

Generally, seniors are not like baby boomers. First, they respect expertise. That's good for professionals who know what they are doing, because they can win the respect of seniors. However, if you do not know what you are doing or add no value, then this is bad news because seniors will not budge.

Let me say more about that here. Many financial professionals I meet offer nothing of value. They are merely salespeople, showing potential customers the same product they can buy anywhere—from any brokerage firm, insurance company, or bank. Yet these people think they are doing financial planning. This type of professional is not a professional at all, but a salesperson whose days are numbered.

If you want to capture the lucrative senior audience, you will need a paradigm, a structure, a program, a better idea why investors should do business with you. That does not mean you need a unique product or service, but you do need the right packaging.

Let me give you an example. In 1990, I started managing equity investments using the Dow Dividend Strategy exclusively.[15] I am able to show people that this system has outperformed 89 percent of all mutual funds over the fifteen years ended 12/31/01.[16] I can further show them that they will never own anything but the thirty blue-chip stocks in the Dow Jones Average—names such as IBM, GM, AT&T, Du Pont—companies that they grew up with and respect. Last, I am able to show them how the system significantly outperforms the market (as measured by the S&P 500) in down years.[17] So I am able to show them a systematic plan that better protects their money, provides a superior return, and feels safer than the mutual funds that every other financial "professional" is recommending.

Even though this system is widely known, I am able to show seniors

[15] The Dow Dividend Strategy is well documented in Michael O'Higgins' book, *Beating the Dow,* and is a widely used system by smart financial advisors.

[16] I ranked all funds in the *Morningstar* database that were in existence for fifteen years as of 12/31/01. I then took the returns of the Dow Dividend Strategy (five-stock strategy) over the same period and deducted 1.25 percent annually for management fees and transaction costs (so that I was comparing returns of the strategy and the funds on the same basis). The Dow Dividend Strategy on this basis outperformed 89 percent of all mutual funds in existence for fifteen years.

why it is so superior given their circumstances and psychology. The value I provide to the client is low volatility, superior capital preservation, and emotional comfort. I have packaged the right service with the right benefits for the right market.

So it's not that you need anything unique or proprietary, but you do need a discipline you believe in, facts to back it up, and the ability to show people why it fits their needs better. If you just want to push the hot stock of the week or the annuity with the best sales trip this year, forget working with affluent seniors—they will see through this shallowness.

A word of advice before leaving this chapter: If you want to focus on the senior market, or any market, focus on it *exclusively*. Only then will you develop a mind-set shared by your prospects and know how to pull their emotional triggers. It's extremely difficult to jump between market niches and be equally effective among them. Yes, I know you were taught that diversification is good. But that's not true in your business. Remember the conglomerates of the 1960s? They're gone. Businesses discovered that focus was a key element to success.

When you're really ill, do you go to a generalist or a specialist? If you were filing for divorce, would you go to the attorney whose ad said, "Business litigation, transaction law, estate planning, and divorce," or the attorney whose ad said, "Divorce, our only business"?

Potential clients will be more attracted to you when you are a specialist, and you will be much more effective when you focus on only one type of prospect. Not too long ago, I received a call from a couple who wanted to see me about planning their portfolio. I asked them where they'd

[17] Performance of the Dow Ten Strategy during bear markets:

Year	Standard and Poor's 500	Dow Dividend Strategy Ten
1973	-15	4
1974	-26	-1
1977	-7	-2
1981	-5	8
1990	-3	-8
2000	-9	6
2001	-11	-5
Total	**-76**	2

heard of me. They told me that on their last trip to see their accountant in my building, they had passed my door and read, "Larry Klein, Certified Senior Advisor." They wanted to meet with me because they did not want an advisor who would be constantly buying and selling and recklessly trying to make a killing in the market. They wanted to work with someone who would understand their needs.

You might be surprised to learn that when my clients ask me to assist their children with financial advice, I refer the kids to a friend at another firm. Why? Because I specialize in working with people aged sixty-plus. I have no insight into the minds of forty-five-year-olds or what they want financially. To think I could sell them something anyway would do a disservice to them and to me. They should consult a specialist who works with people who are saving for retirement or college funding. That's not me, and I am wise to turn this business away and maintain a laser focus where I am an expert. I advise you to do the same.

While you may have been counseled to "get to know the children" (so that when the parents die, you will still retain the account), this is poor advice. The kids will take the money and go their own way—to E*trade, to the financial newsletter they receive, to all of the information they can get for free on the Web.

Not long ago, two of my clients wanted to bring their son, who lived out of the area, to meet me. The parents had been long-time clients and had been satisfied with the relationship and their portfolio results. The son, however, wanted to know why they did not own any technology stocks, and couldn't they do better with his plethora of ideas? I had to point out to this know-nothing that his ideas might be great for him but not for his seventy-year-old parents. I do everything I can to stay away from these "know-it-all" children.

Spend your time wisely with seniors, and you will deal with a responsible group who knows you cannot become a millionaire in six months. Become a specialist in your market and a product generalist.

◆

Has focusing on seniors increased your business; if so, by how much?

My sales have increased by 59 percent by working in the senior marketplace.

Do you feel you are more effective with seniors than other groups?

Definitely. [I have] more understanding of the needs to work on their finances than the younger groups. Most are willing to listen to new ideas and are more ready to act on good solutions to their problems.

How did you decide (what were the factors) to focus on seniors?

All the typical answers to this question influenced me long ago. They have the assets and the needs and the time frame to do financial planning.

WILLIAM G. MADERIS
CAMBRIDGE INVESTMENT RESEARCH

◆

Chapter 2 Summary

Seniors comprise a group of affluent, serious investors, who are accustomed to making decisions and experienced with taking responsibility. They are easy to find, responsive to marketing, and offer you multiple opportunities for income. If you take the time to understand seniors' unique psychology and needs, you may find this the easiest group to ever work with you.

3 Senior Psychology

I do not have a degree in psychology, and I have not consulted with a psychologist about this information.

Nor have I ever seen the following information documented. But ask anyone who has dealt with seniors, and they will agree that many seniors share the same psychological tendencies.

The Sample of One

Seniors have been alive for decades, and they have accumulated more experience than those who are younger. Therefore, it's not surprising that they place great weight on their own experience. However, I have noticed this reliance on personal experience can be taken to extremes, and I call this psychological attribute the "sample of one."

Here's an example. I watched a financial planner introduce the concept of equipment leasing to a senior who desired more income. After two minutes of the sales pitch, this person announced, "I had a neighbor in the equipment leasing business, and he says it's risky stuff." The planner then proceeded to explain the various types of equipment and how leasing arrangements could be very low risk. I watched the prospect's attention dissipate as he had already made his decision. His sample of one, his neighbor's opinion, weighed more heavily than all the facts, data, and logic in the world.

Many producers will try to fight this bias with even more logic, evidence, and "proof" for their recommendation. But experienced producers who know about the sample of one will accept it and move on. Experienced producers know that the best way to help prospects is to have them take action. Even if your recommendation is the "best" one, if the prospect is uncomfortable and does not act, then nothing has been accomplished. Experienced producers do not waste time "arguing" the facts. The marketer Herschel Gordon Lewis, himself a senior, says, "Seniors may not have seen everything on this planet, but many of them *think* they've seen everything."

"Don't Give Me What's Best—Give Me What's Comfortable"

In general, seniors are not optimizers; they are "satisfiers." They are not seeking the best financial solution; they are seeking the solution that feels good.

Even when the ideal financial advisor diligently goes about fact finding with the senior prospect, asks the right questions, gets clarification, and presents the best possible solution, he or she can be dismissed with the response, "I'll think about it."

Seniors want to feel good. That means they like to put their money in familiar places, places that feel safe. Therefore, the goal is to make the "best" recommendation: one the prospect will accept. The best recommendation is therefore a synthesis of the right technical advice and the advice your prospect feels good taking. The financial advising business will always require a large dose of making clients feel better, even if the finance text proclaims that there is a "better" solution.

Not long ago, I talked with a colleague who told me about meeting a retired couple who owned an annuity. They had a comfortable estate and no intention to ever use the annuity. He showed them the advantage of converting the annuity to a life insurance policy and how their heirs could benefit. They liked the idea.

Until this point, all of the concepts were familiar—they knew about the annuity, they had some familiarity with estate taxes, and they had owned life insurance before. He then explained that they would hold the life insurance in an irrevocable life insurance trust, and the deal died.

He killed the deal by using four words together that were totally foreign. They had no knowledge of an "irrevocable life insurance trust." Had my colleague had less integrity, he could have probably made the sale, left the life insurance policy in their estate, and exposed it to estate taxes.

Or, had he explained the trust in this more familiar way, I'm sure he would have had the business:

"Folks, we are making this change to benefit your children as you agreed you want to do. And I want to make absolutely sure that they benefit 100 percent. Each of your children is married, is that correct? God forbid one of them would get a divorce, would you want your ex-daughter-in-law to have part of this money, or would you want it to go to your son?

"To protect your children, you can place the life insurance policy in a trust. That will protect it from such unfortunate occurrences like divorce."

I'm positive that if explained in that manner, the trust would have appealed to the prospects. But instead, they received some technical explanation that was unfamiliar and made them uncomfortable. Result: no sale.

Please keep this in mind: With seniors, you won't get a second chance. Before ever mentioning a solution, you must have completed your fact finding 100 percent, which includes the emotional fact finding. (See the questions on page 46 that Michael Masterson recommends.)

Moschis weighs in, "Marketers must take into consideration the older person's declining cognitive abilities, fears, and reluctance to learn about new products, and they should try to present innovations as simply as possible. One strategy for achieving this objective is to relate the new innovation to an existing one the older consumer already uses."[18] Seniors are especially averse to new ideas where their money is concerned.

If you want the sale, relate your presentation to something familiar for your prospect. For example, when explaining the capital protection feature

[18] Moschis, *Gerontographics.*

of an index annuity, you might start out, "Do you know how, when you invest in a certificate of deposit at the bank, your original principal is protected? Well, this annuity has the same feature . . . " (If you use this comparison, be sure to point out that the annuity is not FDIC-insured.) When presenting a financial idea, don't blaze new trails; just go down the well-worn road.

To summarize the lesson as the marketer Herschel Gordon Lewis states it, "The older we get, the more we resist change. . . . To appeal to seniors, a newcomer should avoid the appearance of newness."[19]

Time Frame

Return calls quickly and respond quickly. Retired prospects' or clients' schedules are not as cramped as yours. You may think it's reasonable to return all calls within twenty-four hours, but many retirees will consider anything over an hour too long.

If your assistant takes the call and says you are on the other line, the senior assumes that when you finish that call, you will call back—and waits for your call. He or she has no idea you have a proposal due later that day, your hard drive has just crashed, you just got a referral to a million-dollar account, and the bank called to say that your business is now in an overdraft position and you'd better get down to the bank.

This incompatibility of time frames is easily remedied. Here are two ideas.

How to Manage Senior Clients' Expectations

1. If you cannot return the call within an hour, have your assistant return the call and tell the prospect that you are tied up until a specific time and that you will call back by a specific time. Then do not be late with this scheduled call.
2. Block out times during the day when you'll return calls. When a call comes in, your assistant can set a phone appointment. (My

[19] Herschel Gordon Lewis. *Silver Linings* (Chicago, IL: Bonus Books Inc., 1996).

> assistant also sets an alarm for me on my computer.) That way, you can manage the prospect's expectation. It's okay if you don't call back in an hour, as long as your clients don't expect you to do so and know you will serve them at a specific time later that day.

I learned about this issue early in my career from two clients. One came to my office to show me that his statement had arrived in an unsealed envelope. He badgered me about my firm needing to be more careful and that his privacy was at risk because the postal carrier could have seen his statement, etc.

This client was not an unreasonable person and had been financially successful. He was in no way an "oddball" or "kook." He simply had enough time on his hands to obsess about an issue that would have gone unnoticed by someone engaged in other personally significant concerns. He never stopped to consider if anything could be done. He was so focused on this occurrence from his point of view that I am certain he never considered that his statement is one of two million prepared in a vast concrete building with people earning minimum wage to operate machines that process ten thousand statements per hour.

Another client stopped in to chat and announced he was on the way to the utility company to pay his bill. I asked why he would waste such time. Why not mail the payment? "What else do I have to do?" he replied.

Of course, it's not that retirees sit around and have nothing to do. Most are active, busy, and aware individuals. But compared to the intensely time-pressured, frantic schedules maintained by many financial professionals, these retirees have an abundance of time, which fosters demanding expectations about your responsiveness. But I will accept this demand anytime over a demand from a younger client that my investment recommendations beat the S&P 500 every year.

In a study by Prince and Associates of why investors changed financial advisors, "Nearly 96 percent were very happy with their portfolio's performance. They were dissatisfied with the service they received and the relationship with their advisor."[20] In my experience, seniors are more sensitive to the service issue than any other market segment.

Big Is Better

Many seniors have discount brokerage accounts. By my count, most of them are at Charles Schwab & Co. As most financial professionals know, Schwab's rates are high, often 100 to 350 percent higher than "deep" discount brokers or online brokerages. The services Schwab provides (research or twenty-four-hour trading) are also available from competing firms. Then why is Schwab, with its higher rates and commodity services, the favorite choice? Because Schwab is big and feels safe.

Schwab advertises a lot. It is one of the oldest discount brokers. And seniors gladly will pay significantly more for a commodity service to feel good. Never mind that any other discount broker has every account insured to $500,000 with SIPC and an additional $9.5 million of private insurance. Never mind that every other discount broker is subject to the same scrutiny and regulation of the NASD. These facts simply do not matter when Schwab feels so good.

What does this mean to the financial professional? If you work for a lesser known firm or have your own practice, you start at a disadvantage. You will need to create the same level of comfort your senior prospect has when he or she considers doing business with Schwab, Hancock, Prudential, Merrill, or some other household name.

Seniors trust big institutions, and they trust authorities. As noted in *Rocking the Ages,* a report on generational marketing, "Matures developed a strong trust in institutions because it was these institutions, like government and big business, that solved the depression and won World War II and the War in Korea."[21] As to authorities, the report states, "Experts were in demand

[20] "CLAS Acts," *Financial Planning Magazine,* March 2000.

for their advice and guidance. From Einstein to Dr. Spock, expert opinion was the determining authority."[22]

How can you compete if you don't work for a big institution? How can you compete when you're not an "expert"?

You can reveal the facts and educate the prospect to the distinctions and advantage of doing business with you. You can easily turn your independent status to your advantage. But you must do it as education, not as a sales pitch. Here's an example from my own practice. I sell long-term care insurance as an independent broker. I have no large name on my business card, yet I easily compete with those captive agents representing large, well-known insurers. It's done like this.

TURNING INDEPENDENT-BROKER STATUS TO ADVANTAGE

"Mr. Jones, I should explain what's different about me from other people you may have talked to about this insurance. Let me ask you a question—when you go to the Chevrolet car dealer, what type of car will you leave with?"

Mr. Jones replies, "A Chevrolet, of course."

"Exactly," I confirm. "The salespeople will not listen and understand your needs and then make the best recommendation. They will sell you their product because that's all they have, the product from their company. When it comes to insuring your health, do you want a sales pitch or do you want the best independent and expert advice?"

"I want the best advice," says Mr. Jones.

"Great. Then I think we can work together because I am an independent agent. I do not represent any particular company. Instead, I have studied the major long-term care policies on the

[21] J. Walker Smith and Ann Clurman. *Rocking the Ages, The Yankelovich Report on Generational Marketing* (New York, NY: Harper Business, 1997). Matures are defined by the authors as those born between 1909 and 1945. At the time of this book, these people would range from fifty-five to ninety-one. This is a slightly broader group than the focus of this book, investors age sixty to seventy-nine.

[22] Ibid.

market. Based on what I have learned, my job is to help you determine the coverage you need, select the companies that will give you the best deal, compare the prices, and select the best policy. I can show you the policies from companies whose names you will recognize, as well as some others of equal size and stability that may be new to you, and then help you make the best choice for your needs. How does that sound?"

Mr. Jones is convinced. "That's exactly what I want—good advice. I don't want a sales pitch."

With this opening, I have now insulated myself against competition from the captive agents at the big insurance companies. The prospect has now made a distinction in his mind between the salesperson (the captive agent) and the independent "expert" advisor. I have overcome the issue of not working for a big institution (which the prospect would normally prefer). I have positioned myself as an expert because I have studied many policies in the market. (I have also written a fifteen-page booklet, "Avoid Mistakes in Buying Long-Term Care Insurance," which establishes me as an expert before we even meet. See the Appendix for information on how to get this booklet personalized for yourself.) I have the capacity and distinctions to compare and contrast different alternatives—and isn't this what experts do?

Please note that this positioning must be done in the beginning of the relationship, not as a response to an objection during the close. You can't position yourself as the independent expert later; it must be done in the beginning of the sales process.

(There are some additional ways to position yourself as an expert—by getting your writing published, and by giving public seminars. We will cover these issues in chapter 8, "Position Yourself As an Expert." Please note that you will not need to write anything—you can publish what others write for you.)

By the way, if you are a captive agent for a large, well-known company, your presentation will stress the size and solidity of your company.

STRESSING SIZE AND SOLIDITY

"Mr. Jones, I've been with ABC for eight years. You've heard of ABC, haven't you?"

"Of course," he agrees. "Who doesn't know ABC? Strong as a rock, right?"

"I guess you're right. The company is now 130 years old, we have $400 billion dollars in assets, and we are the fourth largest financial company in the world. When purchasing insurance, is that the kind of stability that makes you feel comfortable?"

Whether you work independently or for a financial megafirm, you can win the business. You just need to know that the prospect already has a bias toward what's comfortable (big institutions and experts). Address these issues early to solidify your position as you make your presentation. Play your strong suit: If you're captive, sell the solidity and comfort of your big employer. If you're independent, sell the fact that you're the independent expert. In other words, do not dwell on what you do not have (products, credentials, degrees, etc.); instead, make what you do have your trump suit.

"I Don't Want to Make More (Just Help Me Protect What I've Got)"

The financial professional aged thirty to fifty is probably interested in *building* an estate, and it's only natural to project that goal on our senior prospects. However natural it may be, it is highly inaccurate and counterproductive. Unfortunately, the assumption that other people necessarily share our aspirations has wasted millions of dollars in direct mail campaigns, advertisements, and lost sales opportunities.

Imagine you no longer have a paycheck. Your income comes largely from sources you cannot control (social security, pensions, interest). Would you be concerned about making more or protecting your financial lifeline?

Most seniors are less interested in making more than in protecting what they have. And the richer the prospect, the truer this statement. Tim Shoecraft has firsthand experience. He is chairman of Professional Financial Services, LLC, and one of the nation's leading authorities on using life insurance for discounted capital transfers. He personally sells insurance to some of the wealthiest people in the country. His biggest problem? Getting insurance carriers to sell big enough policies. Often, his clients are happy to take a $50- to $100-million policy. Tim's problem is that insurers don't want that much exposure on one person. Compare this to most producers' problem: closing the $1-million policy and convincing clients they "need that much" insurance. The point—the richer they are, the more motivated they are to protect what they have.

WHAT SENIOR PROSPECTS NEED TO SEE

1. Show them the mutual fund that is less volatile (not the one that earns more).
2. Show them the safer annuity company.
3. Show them how to reduce income taxes and keep more.
4. Show them how long-term care insurance will protect their assets and retain their independence.
5. Show them the stocks with the lower beta.

If you want to win in the senior market, make sure the foundation of your communication is about asset protection, reducing risk, diversification, safety, protecting the nest egg, leaving something to the grandkids, and living a financially comfortable life today. You can sum it up in two words: *financial security*.

Here's an example comparing two approaches. I purchased an annuity marketing system that suggested running ads with wording such as "Earn 7 Percent Tax Deferred!" and "CD Rolling Over? Get More Interest." These ads were ineffective. Why? Because they appealed to the desire to earn more rather than the desire to protect principal. I developed a marketing system with ads that appealed to the desire to protect principal, and established myself as an annuity expert. The result: More than a thousand other financial professionals and I are now using these ads and selling a lot more annuities.

Conformity

Seniors do not want to be trendsetters. They like the comfort of doing what everyone else does. Have you noticed that seniors like to travel in groups and join clubs? They have a high need to do as others do.

Have you ever given estate-planning advice and noticed that your prospects were reluctant to implement it? Since most people do their serious estate planning once, the ideas you explain are new to them. They go home reluctant to take action. But if, next week at the bridge club, they hear that two of their friends have drawn living trusts and bought survivorship policies to offset estate taxes, they'll be right back in your office in a heartbeat to proceed. Once they see others doing what you've proposed, the hesitancy drops away. The need to conform is strong.

In fact, I will make a prediction. As I write this in early 2000, the last statistics I evaluated showed that 10 percent of people aged over sixty-five own long-term care policies. Since CNA first introduced long-term care insurance in 1956, it has taken us forty-four years to penetrate 10 percent of the market. However, there is now enough "critical mass" that everyone aged over sixty-five probably knows someone who has a policy. No longer will your prospects be the first ones on the block to take action. Rather, they can more comfortably conform to their peers who have already been doing so. Therefore, I predict that in the next five years, the insurance industry will penetrate at least 25 percent of the market. In other words, the industry will be more successful in the next five years than it has been in the past forty-four—all because conformity is such a strong motivator for seniors.

How do you put this to use in your own business?

When meeting with prospects, tell them, "You're not alone. I have helped three other retired couples take this exact same action this month." Let them know others are doing what you are advising. Or share a statistic about how many people have taken such an action: "Mrs. Jones, I understand that you don't have any friends who have a long-term care policy. But look at this chart. Over five million people have purchased this protection because they see how important it is. Do you think five million people would have made an investment that wasn't a good one?"

Never make recommendations of newly introduced products or services if you want success (unless you are dealing with a prospect from the small fraction of seniors who want to be trendsetters). Show your prospects that their actions will be consistent with the actions of others who have gone before them. Show them how others have profited by taking the same steps.

To summarize, the *Rocking the Ages* report states,

> *Matures developed this unity by conforming to a larger system of values that emphasized hard work as its own reward, financial security through savings, the good of the group before that of the individual, and a belief that the good life had to be earned. Though Matures have always had to sacrifice to meet the demands of this conformity, they have always succeeded. For them, therefore, conformity and fitting in have been linked to success.*[23]

"I Earned It."

Seniors busted their butts to make America what it is. They went hungry during the depression and worked sixteen-hour days for paltry wages. Then, as the country moved out of its economic depression, they got sent off to war, defending the flag. In the three decades after WWII, they worked hard to give their children the college education they couldn't afford for themselves and didn't have an opportunity to pursue. Ask any group of seniors, and they will tell you their objective is for their children to have it easier than they did.

[23] Smith and Clurman, *Rocking the Ages*.

But now, with the kids grown, they want to spend responsibly on themselves. Just look at the boom in cruise travel by seniors, and leisure spending in general. Take a look at the increase in sales of luxury cars. You can see that seniors are now realizing they've earned it!

How does this impact the financial professional? Particularly in the arena of estate planning, you're doomed if you cannot show people what's in it for them. If you show your senior prospects you can save their kids $1 million in estate taxes but it's going to cost $20,000 a year starting now, you'll be making a lot of pitches before you close a sale.

Your client is thinking, *I earned it, so now what's in it for me?* In the arena of estate planning, is it any wonder that devices such as charitable remainder trusts have been successful? It's a way for Mom and Dad to sell their old farmland, defer the capital gains tax, and get a larger income. Mom and Dad get an immediate benefit. But try and sell a survivorship policy to parents who are not already making gifts to their kids, and you'll do a lot of talking without much action.

There are some legal devices that will help answer the "What's in it for me?" objection when attempting to sell insurance for estate taxes. We'll cover those in chapter 7, "Important Products and Services for the Senior Market."

As a last recommendation, you will do well to speak of estate planning in ways that will benefit the grandchildren, not the children. As far as I have observed, today's seniors were very motivated to get their children a college education and a good start. But once they saw their children become adults, they were a lot less likely to keep them on the family "payroll." However, the grandchildren have now taken the children's place in the checkbooks of today's seniors. In fact, seniors make 25 percent of toy purchases.[24]

Familiarity

It's no surprise that it takes someone over sixty longer than someone younger to learn a new language, play a new game, or operate a computer. You can make faster inroads when communicating with seniors, especially

[24] Smith and Clurman, *Rocking the Ages.*

with new information, by obeying the rule of familiarity. Bridge any new idea to what's already familiar to your senior prospect.

In explaining a recommended bond, for example, relate the bond to a CD at the bank. (Of course, make the distinction about the CD being FDIC-insured while the bond is not.) But relate the fact that the bond pays off face value at maturity, just like the CD. The interest rate is fixed, just like the CD. The term is for a preset fixed period, just like the CD. Such comparisons will aid the understanding of a new investment idea or financial concept.

I encourage you to carry this familiarity concept to its ultimate advantage. For example, I have my office on the main, most familiar street in town. When I hold seminars, I hold them at established restaurants that have been in town for twenty years or more. My clients' portfolios are all centered around blue-chip stocks, familiar names such as Caterpillar, Du Pont, AT&T, J. P. Morgan, and General Motors.

In familiarity there is comfort. Always select a familiar reference point when starting your relationship to help build comfort and trust quickly.

"But I Read That . . ."

Seniors have a lot of respect for what they read and what's produced by the media. Remember that for much of their impressionable years, there was no television. Radio and newspaper were the authoritative sources. Those who lived through the depression read a lot because there was no money for other forms of entertainment. As a result, books and newspapers, and the people who write them, are respected authorities.

How many times have you had a client call and say, "I read in the newspaper that . . ." or have a prospect say the same in the middle of your presentation. They want to pit your knowledge against that of a newspaper reporter. In the senior's mind, the reporter may have more credibility than you simply because writers are seen as experts.

You'll learn more later on how you too can become a writer and expert. For now, be aware that this is an issue you will need to handle.

Referrals

Referrals are typically obtained from people who share their experiences with others. Seniors may be a little disappointing in that regard.

While there are segments of the senior population who discuss finances with their friends, many seniors were raised with the notion that you do not talk about money matters with others. Morgan and Levy reveal, " . . . Almost a quarter of the population over fifty (23 percent) avoids a professional financial advisor because they want to keep their financial affairs private."[25]

If such a significant portion of people over fifty do not even want to disclose their financial affairs to a professional, it's doubtful that they talk about financial issues with their friends. If financial discussions are absent from their conversation, there's not much chance these people will be mentioning your name.

The best chance you have for referrals is to provide excellent service and keep in touch at least quarterly. One other tactic I use is, when I open a new account, I send a gift basket with goodies and several business cards. When the client calls to thank me, I say, "Don't eat all of those goodies yourself. Share them with the neighbors and give them one of my business cards."

Trust—The Central Issue

One very positive issue selling into the senior market is that decisions are made based largely on trust. Unlike a baby boomer with a prove-it-to-me attitude (e.g., "Why should I pay your fee?" "Why is your product better?" "Why shouldn't I just do this myself?"), seniors decide to move forward based on trust.

◆

Seniors look for relationship, trust, someone to talk to—then concepts and products. Other markets look for concepts and products first then everything else. I am more effective with seniors because I sell myself first.

BRIAN KELLY, FINANCIAL ADVISOR

◆

[25] Morgan and Levy, *Segmenting the Mature Market.*

Here's what Morgan and Levy found in their research about why seniors do or don't do business with financial advisors:

> *Cost aside, three reasons for not going to a professional for financial planning focus on the relationship between the client and the planner. They all relate to trust. Based on other research we have conducted, we believe that developing trust is central to the sale of financial products and services.*[26]

Is it any wonder that financial salespeople or companies that take a product orientation may be finding it hard to compete? Based on the above, it becomes a requirement that successful selling to seniors revolves around the relationship that the salesperson creates, while product features, financial returns, or even understanding how their money gets invested, is less important.

Therefore, it is best that new people in the business, advisors with little training, product-focused salespeople, and salespeople with only a narrow understanding of the senior market stay out of it. They will have trouble creating the necessary trust to make significant sales.

How to Create Trust and Credibility With Seniors

Fortunately, creating trust and gaining credibility is not about possessing credentials, degrees, or a great investment track record. Creating trust and gaining credibility is not about what you have; it's about what you do. Pay attention to these aspects of your behavior and you will build trust more quickly and make more sales.

◆

> *Become the clients' friend first and develop their trust. Let them talk about their family. Show them you are truly interested in their needs. Ask for their commitment to purchase from you up front. They respect that and honor it.*
>
> **WILSON KONE,** FINANCIAL ADVISOR

◆

[26] Morgan and Levy, *Segmenting the Mature Market.*

Your Language

When you speak, never use jargon. I define jargon as language that is not within everyday, common usage. For example, I never use the phrase *variable annuity* because it's jargon. Instead, I say "an annuity whose value goes up and down with the financial markets." I never use *S&P 500;* I say, "an index of the five hundred largest companies in America." You will need to police yourself rigorously because there are phrases you use every day that you do not think of as jargon, but they are foreign words to your prospects. And each time you use a term your prospect does not understand, your chance of doing business decreases.

Let me show you how insidious this problem really is. Do you have a credential after your name such as CFP, CLU, ChFC, RIA, or other acronym? For some reason, you assume prospects know what that credential means. They do not. They have no clue what a CFP is, or even what a Certified Financial Planner does. I know that the CFP Board would not be happy with my assertion, but next time you're in a group of people, ask them what CFP means. See how accurate they are. Therefore, at every opportunity—in your promotional materials, your seminar handouts, your biographical page—you must remove the jargon or explain it.

SAMPLE EXPLANATION OF CREDENTIALS

Joe Johnson is a Certified Financial Planner. This required Joe to complete two years of courses covering major aspects of financial planning and pass six tests and a two-day, ten-hour exam proving his knowledge in the arenas of taxes, investments, and estate planning.

Once you start communicating clearly by eliminating all jargon or explaining it when you must use it, you will gain trust because people will now understand you. There will be no gaps between your speaking and other people's understanding. The job of being 100 percent clear is yours—you cannot expect anyone to ever tell you, "I do not understand you." Rather than tell you this, people just leave and never become clients.

Knowledge

Let's face it, whether you sell securities or insurance, the test you passed to get your license did not make you knowledgeable enough to serve clients well.

You need to know your craft. If you don't have the knowledge you need, then get into classes or train yourself. You will not fool anyone. Worse, you run the risk of getting sued. Knowledge includes both technical knowledge and product knowledge. In the appendix is a list of educational companies and methods to become more technically competent.

Ability to Explain and Answer Clearly

I talk with people all day long. It amazes me that about 20 percent of the time when I ask a question, I get an answer to a different question. Do you ever respond to your prospects' questions with answers to entirely different questions?

Simple cure: Let them finish asking the question. Repeat it to ensure you understood. Then answer. Remember, if you are forty-five years old, the question you think you would ask is not necessarily the question the seventy-year-old asks. Listen, repeat, answer.

◆

> *I really enjoy working with seniors. I had always worked in the personal, rather than business, market because I like the rapport that develops with clients. I find the seniors very easy to work with—I try to be very straightforward with them, and I think they appreciate that.*
>
> **SHARON BERRY,** FINANCIAL ADVISOR

◆

◆

> *Ninety-eight percent of my business is with seniors. I have always focused on seniors [because they] are more effective and they are better decision makers. They have less ego problems, and they are used to dealing with professionals. They have not been sold the message by the media that they don't need an advisor. Also, they are not looking for 45 percent returns every year, so they*

are more in line with my style.

NEAL FRANKLE, CFP

◆

Following Through and Managing Expectations

Do what you say you will: Be on time, send the item you promised, call when you said you would, etc. If you do not keep your word meticulously, seniors will not do business with you. There is no fudge factor for them.

If a friend shows up ten minutes late, you might think nothing of it. For seniors, your word is who you are. If you do not do exactly what you say, you are not to be trusted. Notice that seniors are always on time (and even early) for their appointments, and they expect the same from you. If you are running late, then you must call and tell them so.

Ability to Relate Services and Products to Seniors' Psychological Wants

As mentioned previously, seniors are motivated to preserve capital so they can feel comfortable and secure about their finances and be assured of their financial and physical independence. If you emphasize other aspects of your product or services (e.g., high return, lowest cost), seniors will sense that you really do not understand them, and they will not become clients.

For example, it would seem that anyone would be attracted to an investment with high returns. So the inexperienced salesperson might stress the great track record of the mutual fund she is touting. But seniors often have capital preservation as their primary goal. And since many people already know the adage, "The higher the return, the higher the risk," an existing investment track record could very well be a deal killer.

Credentials

Credentials receive an undue emphasis. Many advisors ask me about which credentials they should get as if it would make a significant impact in their business. Yet credentials do not make that much of a difference.

That said, credentials do help. The one professional title that says more plainly than any other that you are serious about the senior market is Certified Senior Advisor. This designation is awarded by the Society of Senior Certified Advisors in Denver. At this writing, approximately 8,000 advisors hold this credential and 200 more become CSAs each month.

To become a CSA, you need to attend a weeklong class and take an exam, plus provide evidence of continuing education each year. The Society provides nice brochures, which simply state why any senior would want to do business with a CSA above others.

While any pertinent credential and education are worthwhile, the CSA designation is the one I recommend for professionals serious about the senior market. Details can be obtained by use of the form provided in the appendix.

Chapter 3 Summary

Understanding senior psychology is simply being aware that seniors think differently than you do and policing yourself from imposing your values onto your senior prospects. Although the psychological issues in this chapter are common to many in the senior market, every prospect is an individual. So, when in doubt about what's going on in their heads, just ask and listen.

4 Advertising to Seniors: What Works and What Doesn't

You may be a salaried person in the marketing department of a large insurance company.

Or you may be a financial planner who creates sales letters and marketing materials and lives and dies by the commissions and fees you generate. In either case, this chapter will help you avoid advertising that bombs and give you the building blocks for writing winning copy for the senior market.

Much advertising to the senior market is ineffective. The Life Insurance Marketing Research Association (LIMRA) agrees:

> *Analysts have found that marketing programs for mature adults fail more frequently than those directed at other age groups. This is partially because advertisers don't know how to draw them into their ads.*[27]

First, it's important to know why much advertising to seniors does *not* work. Once we see the mistakes, it becomes much easier to employ the right tactics.

Let's think about the people who write advertising: They work for ad agencies and are not retired. So we have a whole army of advertising creators, none of whom have any personal experience of what it feels like to be retired. In addition, these people spend their day talking to each

[27] LIMRA. *Meeting the Needs of the Mature Market*, 1996.

other, not to retirees. Any stockbroker or life insurance agent prospecting in the senior market probably has a lot more insight into what motivates a senior prospect to action than an advertising expert sitting on the twenty-third floor of a Madison Avenue office building. The advertising expert's exposure to senior thinking may be the sum total of a three-hour focus group with seniors conducted the week before. What's more, this person's professional field of study was journalism or advertising, not finances. What he or she knows about annuities was learned from two brochures read over lunch.

According to Moschis, as quoted in *American Demographics*,

> *A lot of business decisions are based upon misconceptions about the older consumer. When you have ad directors in their thirties, it's hard for them to create ads for people in their sixties and seventies.*[28]

Do you see why much of senior advertising produced by financial firms doesn't generate a very profitable result? It's being developed by people who have no clue!

Richard Leventhal, editor of the *Journal of Consumer Marketing*, recounts a *New York Times* article reporting on a 1995 survey about older people:

WHAT DO PEOPLE THINK ABOUT THE ELDERLY?

- Forty-six percent of the respondents felt most older people could not adapt to change.
- Fifty percent said that most older people lived below the poverty line.
- More than 65 percent agree with the statement that most older people say they are lonely.
- Seventy-five percent agreed that at least one of ten older people lives in a long-term care institution.[29]

[28] Pol, et al. *American Demographics*..

[29] Richard C. Leventhal. "Aging Consumers and Their Effects on the Marketplace," *Journal of Consumer Marketing*, 14, no. 4 (1997): 276.

None of these statements are correct, but they do represent the attitudes that make for ageism. Why are perceptions so far off? Why have we failed to set the record straight? Why does our advertising continue to show old people as ancient, twisted, limping people in wheelchairs or with canes, wrinkled and covered with gray hair, or with no hair at all? Is this why marketers have ignored the emerging mature markets? There is an obvious marketing opportunity here for us.

Specifically, ineffective senior advertising commits the following crimes.

Mistake #1: Emphasizing Opportunities, Returns, and Greed

Most advertising focuses on an opportunity to make more money or a higher return, or it attempts in some other way to appeal to greed. Seniors, however, are motivated to preserve their capital and reduce risk. They are far more interested in keeping what they have. If we continue to advertise "opportunities," we will continue to waste a lot of money on ineffective ads.

For example, which headline do you think will get more attention from seniors?

LEARN HOW TO DOUBLE YOUR MONEY
IN THE STOCK MARKET

or

THREE WAYS YOU COULD LOSE A FORTUNE
IN THE STOCK MARKET—IN THE NEXT 90 DAYS!

You will always get more response from an ad to seniors that addresses their needs.

What Advertising Should Promise Seniors

- Preserve what you have.
- Avoid outliving your money.
- Be safer.
- Retain financial independence.

Mistake #2: Using a Logical Rather than Emotional Approach

All good advertising has an emotional appeal, yet many financial advertisements still appeal to a non-emotional benefit. Compare the following factual headline to the emotional headline:

You Can Use the Equity in Your Home
to Increase Your Income

or

Here's How Mrs. Mary Jones, Social Security Recipient,
Buys Her Grandchildren All the Toys They Want
for Christmas

If you do not offer an emotional benefit, your response will be weak. Show your prospects how the benefit will make them feel, and personalize it if you can. If you are sending direct mail, the ultimate personalization is possible with mail merge. How about using this title on your letter:

How Mary Jones Can Enjoy a 10-Day
Bahamas Cruise this Winter

You may find such a title strange for selling a financial product. But that's the point of why so much financial advertising is so ineffective. We keep selling product features and not consumer benefits. Mrs. Jones wants to know how she will benefit (e.g., a cruise to warm places when it's cold) rather than just being offered an increase in her income.

Mistake #3: Using a Statistical Rather than Personal Approach

We baby boomers think statistics are sacred. We grew up watching the first mission to the moon and learned that if the trajectory had been off by only an inch, the rocket would have missed the moon by hundreds of miles. We think this type of scientific precision is of interest or importance to everyone. But it's rarely appropriate for advertising. Consider this boring headline I have seen hundreds of times (based on a 1991 *New England Journal of Medicine* article that gets used as the rallying cry of the long-term care insurance industry):

FORTY-THREE PERCENT OF PEOPLE OVER AGE SIXTY-FIVE WILL SPEND TIME IN A NURSING HOME

The following headline would be much more effective if we want our senior reader's attention:

MRS. JOHNSON, AGE SEVENTY-TWO, JUST SPENT HER LAST DOLLAR TO PAY HER NURSING HOME BILL

Seniors are scared about losing their financial and physical independence. When you appeal to that and can show a solution, you will get a much greater response than by repeating what you think are compelling statistics.

Mistake #4: Transferring Your Motivations to the Senior Market

Whatever you think is "good" or "bad" is worthless when it comes to advertising to the senior market. As indicated above, if you're forty years old, doubling your money in the stock market may be of interest to you. To many seniors, this sounds too risky, so they have little interest. To advertise effectively, you need to get your ego and your arrogance out of the way. Just look at how the following advertising headlines or tag lines can alienate the senior audience:

LEARN THREE WAYS TO INCREASE YOUR INCOME!

(You think, *Learning is good; everyone wants to learn.* Seniors think, *I'm not interested in a course or the drudgery of learning; I finished school long ago—just tell me what I need to know.*)

NEW WAYS TO PROFIT FROM FIXED INCOME INVESTMENTS

(You think, *Something NEW will surely attract attention and give me an edge.* Seniors think, *It's new? Great, let someone else be the guinea pig and call me when it's proven.*)

HIGH RETURN FROM ANNUITIES

(You think, *Seniors surely want a high return.* Seniors think, *High return equals high risk. No, thank you!*)

Let me summarize the major point of this section on advertising to seniors, or any market: Never assume your market's motivations are your own. You must spend plenty of time listening to your prospects. You need to identify their most powerful emotions, negative and positive, and their greatest fears and aspirations.

In Michael Masterson's course on copy writing[30], he states that you have to know who you are talking to.

ASK YOURSELF THESE QUESTIONS

- Who are my prospects?
- How old are they?
- What do they look like?
- How do they think?
- What do they read?
- What scares them?
- What excites them?
- What are their likes and dislikes?

[30] Michael Masterson. *Accelerated Program For Six-Figure Copy Writing* (self-study course).

APPEAL TO THESE EMOTIONS WITH SENIORS

Once you really know your prospect, you can appeal to the following emotions. I have ranked these in the order in which I observe seniors are most responsive.

1. Desire for security
2. Need to be wanted
3. Fear
4. Pride
5. Guilt
6. Vanity
7. Greed

ADVERTISING FOR SENIORS: THE BASICS

Below is a list of advertising motivators I have compiled in working with seniors for fifteen years. These are motivators that impact the majority of the senior market. But, as with any market niche, there are subniches with their own motivators. If you are marketing to a subniche (e.g., retired real estate developers), you will need to develop your own list.

1. Protection of capital is superior to increasing wealth (in other words, return *of* principal is more important than return *on* principal).
2. Something proven is better than something new.
3. A face-to-face conversation is better (more reliable, more trustworthy) than a telephone conversation.
4. Conservatism wins—clean-shaven men with suits and ties, women in dresses, a firm handshake, using respectful titles of Mr. and Mrs.

(Continued on next page.)

5. The relationship, how much your senior prospects trust you, is ALWAYS more important than how much they understand about the investment.
6. Consistency, proof that you have staying power, is a huge marketing plus (you run the same seminar *every month,* you show up at church *every week,* your radio spot is on *every morning,* they see you *every time* they come to the bank).
7. Items in writing are credible, *especially* if printed in the newspaper. So always give a brochure or put your proposal in writing. Do not assume your prospect reads it, but you must provide it.
8. Eliminate all jargon and never attempt to confuse (assuming the prospect will then need your help). Clarity is the key to a big response.

Chapter 4 Summary

If the financial services industry continues to communicate to seniors about financial services and products by citing the traditional features and benefits, billions of sales will be lost. This product orientation will not maximize sales into America's wealthiest market. Only customer-focused communication, where we baby boomers learn to speak the concerns of the senior market, will maximize our opportunity to capture the real sales potential.

The banking industry is failing in the sales of reverse mortgages. The life industry is failing with sales of life insurance and sluggishly penetrating the long-term care opportunity in the senior market. The securities industry has no strategy or channel of communication for the senior market and also continues its product/service focus rather than customer focus. However, financial firms and producers can profitably target the senior market by employing the emotionally based, customer focused tactics in this chapter.

The remainder of the book explains how the individual financial producer, as well as financial firms, can thrive in the senior market by adjusting the communication and psychology employed in reaching seniors.

5 Marketing to Seniors:

In the last chapter, we looked at advertising, which includes writing the copy that motivates seniors, and the headlines and text that appeal to their psychology and emotions.

In this chapter, we want to look at how to employ that message in advertising campaigns, direct mail, and seminars.

To the degree you are successful at marketing, you can do less prospecting and chasing of prospects. The right marketing does not need to be expensive, but it needs to be smart. The right marketing will ensure that you have a full calendar of appointments and that you have as many prospects as you want.

The underlying theme in successful senior marketing must resonate with their perceived scarcity. Put yourself in the shoes of someone who is seventy years old. Time is scarce. Money is scarce. (They may have plenty, but they perceive it as scarce because they cannot earn any more should they lose it.) Good health may be scarce.

If your marketing speaks to helping them with these scarcity issues, you will have all the new clients you want.

Marketing Campaigns

You need marketing programs that produce a continuous flow of prospects each month. In my practice, we do monthly seminars. In addition, we run one or more direct-response programs that offer free educational booklets. These booklets reveal the most common errors seniors make when investing. Titles include these:

ANNUITY OWNER MISTAKES

AVOID MISTAKES IN BUYING LTC INSURANCE

MISTAKES IN SELECTING MUTUAL FUNDS

Our booklets attract the clients we want and can help: people looking to learn more and improve their financial situations. If we desire more clients, we simply hold more seminars or run more advertisements for the booklets. (The appendix provides additional information on these booklets.)

Advertising does work, and producers using our direct response advertising system throughout the United States earn anywhere from $5,000 to $30,000 monthly from a system that takes about fifteen hours a month to implement.

The Ad Must Appear in Publications That Target the Senior Audience

Forget about using the daily newspaper unless you live in a small town or have a very large budget. Senior publications include public publications (e.g., those that gain their revenue by selling ads and thus are looking for advertisers) or private publications (those issued by groups, associations, and clubs). You can obtain a list of public senior publications by ordering (or finding at the library) the *Senior Media Directory* [Creative Ink, (612) 894-6720]. Private senior publications require more looking, as these publications are not in the business of selling ad space but will accept ads occasionally.

Private publications include and can be found through newsletters and bulletins of nonprofit associations such as senior travel clubs, garden clubs, associations such as the Retired Teachers Association, or the National Association of Retired Federal Employees. These associations typically have chapters across the United States with their own local publications. Here's how you find them.

SOURCES FOR SENIOR ASSOCIATIONS

1. In the county and state section of your telephone directory white pages, look for the agency that services seniors. They often maintain a listing of senior organizations in your area.
2. In the yellow pages, look under the headings *Associations* and *Senior Associations.*
3. Watch your daily newspaper for the weekly listing of club meetings or calendar of events. You will see meetings of senior groups listed with a phone number to call and learn about advertising opportunities.
4. Ask your senior clients what clubs and organizations they belong to or what publications they receive that are targeted at the senior or retiree market.
5. The retirees of large companies (e.g., Fortune 1000) often form independent retirees associations with their own newsletters or bulletins. Most accept ads. Call the human resources department of the local company offices to find the retiree organization.
6. Your local library should have a directory of newsletters and associations (Gales or Ulrichs).
7. Religious and ethnic organizations (churches and church organizations, synagogues, the Jewish Federation, etc.) often produce publications, and although these are not targeted at the senior market, the majority of the readers are often seniors. So do

not look at the title of a publication to decide if it's a senior publication. You need to call the publication and get their reader demographics.

8. Call your local chapter of the American Association of Retired Persons. Although they will not accept your ad, they may maintain a listing of senior organizations in your area. Additionally, they may have a listing of any senior fairs that are held throughout the year. Attend a senior fair, as many of the senior organizations will exhibit there. In just a couple hours, you can uncover plenty of organizations and advertising outlets that you never knew existed.
9. Most major hospitals have a very active senior marketing effort, which includes periodically sending newsletters to seniors in the surrounding community. These newsletters often accept advertising at very favorable rates.

If you live in a small town and do not have the resources listed above, then the daily newspaper may be your only source.

How to Use Daily Newspapers to Best Advantage

1. Ask the publisher what day of the week more seniors read the paper. It may be the day when all of the coupons appear in the paper. That's the day you want to advertise.
2. Run your ad on the financial page or the obituary page. Seniors read these pages most frequently. Test them both.
3. Investigate the cost of doing an insert rather than an advertisement. Many daily newspapers will insert your 8.5" x 11" flyer right in the middle of the publication. These inserts have several advantages over an ad:
   - They are larger, and you can include more copy.

- They are often less expensive than ads.
- You can often select the Zip codes you want to target.
- They are seen by more readers, as the inserts tend to fall into the readers' laps when they open their papers. Therefore, almost everyone sees your flyer, as opposed to your ad on page fourteen that is seen only by people who look at that page.

What Your Ad Should Say

To produce an effective ad, the headline must include some emotionally grabbing copy that will get your prospects to read the entire ad. In the ad, offer something for free, such as a booklet that will help your prospect achieve an emotionally compelling goal. For example, if we know that seniors have a fear of losing financial independence, then a good title for a free booklet or a report would be "How to Avoid the Three Mistakes That Cause Retirees to Lose Their Financial Independence."

The booklet should not only contain some good information, but also your picture and biography. Anything you send must build your credibility and image as an expert.

The prospects can obtain your booklet in two ways: You can have them mail in a coupon or call for it. I have had much better experience asking respondents to call a toll-free phone line that captures their phone number. This allows me and my staff to call, answer any questions, clarify the information, and offer additional assistance.

Calling allows people to respond immediately. (Respondents don't need to look for a pen or envelope or stamp.) In addition, when completing coupons, respondents often omit their phone numbers even when you ask for them.

You must send the booklets out immediately and follow up by phone not more than eight days after you send the booklet. I have found the most powerful call goes something like this: "Mr. Jones? This is Larry Klein. A few days ago you called our office and ordered a booklet on 'Three Ways for Retirees to Avoid Losing Their Financial Independence.' Did you receive it? Great. What motivated you to order the booklet?"

Never ask if someone has read it. Ninety percent of the people will not have read the booklet—and you don't care. The purpose of the booklet is not to educate people, although it would if they read it. The purpose of the booklet is to introduce you, build your credibility as an expert, and precede your first contact so that yours is a warm call.

The key to these calls is to ask relevant questions and get people talking. Explore what motivated them to respond to the booklet offer. Listen carefully, and your prospect will reveal a concern or perceived problem, at which point you can offer a meeting to give them some advice, review an annuity, explain long-term care, bring some articles about estate planning, etc. We use this approach in a highly competitive, affluent senior market and get appointments with 20 percent of the respondents.

How to Test an Ad's Effectiveness

You will know within thirty days if your ad is profitable.

When you select a publication, ask the publisher for the readership study. Make sure the people you want to reach are readers of that publication. For example, when I advertise in a senior publication, I am seeking at least 50 percent readership by those aged sixty-five and older.

Next, *test* your ad. Run the ad *once*. One insertion will give you enough feedback for the test. Let's take an example. You run the ad for a cost of $300. You get ten responses, and you conservatively estimate that you will get one appointment. Your chance of doing business is 70 percent. Your average profit from the sale is $2,000. Let's put it together:

ESTIMATED PROFIT FROM TEN RESPONSES

One appointment x 70 percent probability of sale x $2,000 profit = expected revenue	$1,400
Cost of ad	300
Profit	**$1,100**

This ad has a 4.7 times gross return ($1,400/$300). Therefore, you will keep running this ad. In fact, you will run this ad as long as the ad pays for itself (at least a 1:1 return). How can you make a profit if the ad only pays for itself? Because we have assigned no value to the other nine people who did not set an appointment. If you send them a monthly newsletter, contact them again, invite them to a seminar, etc., some of these people will become clients.

TACTICS TO EMPLOY WHEN PLACING ADS IN A PUBLICATION

1. Tell the advertising rep that you know nothing about the publication. If it works for you, you will run your ad month after month, so you are ready to sign a twelve-month contract (which will give you the lowest rates). However, if the ad does not give good results, they agree to let you out of the contract, and you owe them nothing. The publication will probably tell you that one month is not really a fair test because readers need to see your ad for several months before the ad has its maximum results. Yet, what they'll tell you is not true. I have been advertising for years, and if the publication is good, you will get immediate results. So tell them you want the deal as specified. I have gotten this deal every time.
2. As you put your pen to the contract to sign, say, "By the way, I will be taking the ad agency 15 percent discount." Publications routinely build 15 percent into their ad prices to pay advertising agencies. Since you are not using an agency, you tell the publication you are taking the 15 percent. You can get this from national, as well as local, publications.
3. Tell the publication your ad must appear in the upper right half of the right-hand page (black area on the following illustration). They will tell you that the placement cannot be guaranteed. In my experience, this is a lie. Nicely tell them it's your way or you

cannot advertise.

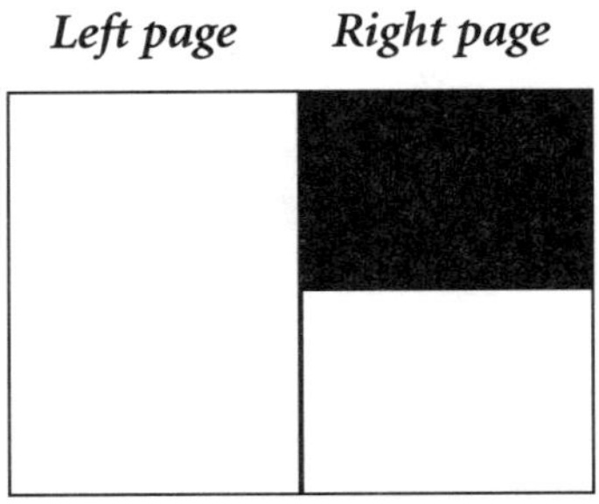

Expect the following: a one-tenth of a percent response rate per month from a targeted publication. So if the publication has a twenty thousand circulation, you should receive about twenty leads each time the ad runs.

Use a separate 800-number for each publication so you can gauge it. Some publications will just be lousy, and you want to know that as soon as possible.

If So Many Direct-Mail Programs Fail, How Can You Beat the Odds and Be Successful?

It's safe to say that many producers in the financial services arena have tried direct mail. Large mutual fund companies are happy to print as many of those tri-fold pieces with your name and address as you want, and you are free to waste your firm's postage or your own money sending them. Insurance companies just love to send direct mail to compensate for their agents' insufficient prospecting. It's a gamble, but the hope is that the agent drops five thousand pieces, gets a 2 percent response and then has one hundred people to call, and maybe has appointments with 20 to 30 percent. If the numbers actually worked like this, it would be great.

I recently coached someone entering the mutual fund business. He was sure that the mutual fund company was making him a great offer. They would personalize the tri-fold brochures with his name and pay for inserting thirty thousand copies in the local newspaper. The respondent would need only to complete a reply card and send it back.

The result? He received eight replies, had one appointment and no sales. This had nothing to do with his lack of sales ability—he had been the number-one salesperson of direct participation programs with his broker dealer.

You've probably tried direct mail or such newspaper inserts at least once and had similar, less than stellar results. After spending hundreds or even thousands of dollars, you may have even come to the conclusion that direct mail doesn't work. Direct mail *does* work, and although there are many components to a successful campaign, I'll cover three critical variables.

Direct mail, done the right way, gets many producers response rates in excess of 3 percent. Any direct mail marketer will tell you that a 2 percent response is fabulous, so anything above 3 percent is highly coveted.

Before we go much further, let me get to the most important issue—keeping your direct mail from getting tossed out. Think about this. What percentage of your mail do you throw away each day? I'll bet it's more than half. In fact, my guess is that you sort through your mail assuming it's mostly garbage, and you look for the one or two pieces to give a few moments' attention. Indeed, most mail is headed for the garbage before recipients even look at it. So as a direct mailer, you have an uphill battle before your piece is even postmarked.

Your first job is to keep the direct mail piece *out* of the garbage can. Therefore, you must know the criteria for what goes to the garbage and what gets retained.

If It Looks Like Junk Mail, It's Headed for the Garbage

- Tri-fold mailers that are obviously bulk-mailed hold no appeal.
- Envelopes with sales pitches printed on them usually remain unopened.
- Envelopes with a return address of ABC Securities or XYZ Insurance Company scream, "Please let us sell you some financial services!"

- Envelopes with carrier sort codes, bar codes, labels, and other items announce, "This same item has been mailed to four million households."

So, how do you distinguish your direct mail?

Mail in plain white window envelopes with a first-class stamp. No bar codes, no carrier route sort, no labels. Your return address should just list your name, not the name of your financial company. Make your direct mail so nondescript that it becomes impossible for the recipient to prejudge the contents. From the look of the envelope, the contents could be a check, a letter from the doctor, or an announcement from the travel club. It's impossible to judge what's inside, which forces your recipient to open the envelope.

Bingo! You succeed where most direct mailers fail: You get the envelope opened. You now have four seconds to get the reader's attention. Now we're ready to talk about the contents.

Avoid Common Mistakes

1. Match Your Message to Your Audience

This sounds like a simple issue, but it's not. Here's an example. A producer sent direct mail targeted to an audience of seniors but trumpeting investments with a high return. The producer felt that seniors generally want more income, so a high return should be attractive. As you've learned, while it's true that many seniors would like to earn more, a high return is not the *emotionally compelling* issue for seniors. Their emotionally compelling issue is preservation of principal. They seek to preserve their estates. And they are skeptical that a high return can also mean high risk. The response was terrible.

Understanding this emotionally compelling issue, an attorney's sole marketing program was to send eight thousand letters each calendar quarter to seniors with home values of $400,000 and above. The letter explained that, without a living trust,

- the family could pay unnecessary taxes,

- the estate could be tied up in probate for months or even years,
- busy children could be bothered by numerous details, and
- attorneys' and executors' fees could easily total $40,000 or more.

The reaction from recipients? This attorney did sufficient business from those mailings to fill his calendar all year! He sold the trust as a vehicle to help preserve their estates.

2. Include a Compelling Title and Subtitles or Bullet Points in the Mailing Piece

While the title (every piece of direct mail must have a big, bold title) must push the audience's primary "hot button," the bullet points help capture those segments of the audience with different agendas.

For example, not all seniors are motivated to preserve their estates. Occasionally, I meet seniors who are intent on *building* their estates. At age seventy, some are still buying property, wheeling and dealing. Or others' main focus is their children. Still others may just hate paying taxes. If you can develop subtitles or bullet points in your mail piece around these issues, you can capture a response from these subgroups or market segments. For example, your headline and some effective bullet points might be as follows.

IS YOUR ESTATE OVER $1 MILLION?
HERE'S HOW THE IRS CAN'T WAIT TO TAKE SOME FROM YOU.

- Three Ways to Keep Your Entire Estate Away from the IRS
- How to Grow Your Real Estate Portfolio and Make It Immune from Estate Tax
- This Simple Move Saves $270,000!

The more bullet points that push those emotionally compelling hot buttons, the bigger your response to the mailing.

These two issues—identifying the primary emotional motivator and identifying the "submotivators"—require that you really know your audience. I invite you to investigate your audience thoroughly even if you think you know them. You can easily do this by calling some of your existing clients in your target group and asking them a few questions.

QUESTIONS TO ASK YOUR EXISTING CLIENTS

- "What's your number-one financial concern?"
- "If your main source of income disappeared tomorrow, who would you be most concerned about?"
- "What's your most important asset?"
- "Twenty years from now, where will your money be?"
- "What do you want to leave your kids? Your grandkids?"
- "If you were president, what two things would you change?"

3. Make a Non-Intimidating Offer

Do not waste your time telling people, "We will call you soon." Instead, ask for action. If you want high-quality prospects, let them make the first move. These are the motivated people. If you keep chasing people, you'll have prospects and eventually clients who need to keep being convinced. Good clients are those who take action, so let the prospect come to you.

Don't ask them to call and schedule a free appointment. That's too intimidating. You are a stranger, they do not know you, and you're asking too much. Instead of asking prospects to schedule a free appointment, do this:

- Offer a free booklet.
- Offer a free class/seminar (where they can remain anonymous).
- Offer free information from a web site (the web site will require them to register).
- Offer a free quote.

Remember the saying, "You can lead a horse to water, but you can't make him drink." It's the same with prospects: You can only lead them and do some gentle nudging. You can't ask for the moon, as in "Call our office for a no-obligation, one-hour financial review."

The subtler offer allows people to take some no-risk action and receive something they perceive has benefit. Once they respond, you have prospects who are worth pursuing for business and who need or have interest in your assistance.

Once in the home, you pursue your fact finding and possibly make a sale or schedule a closing appointment. Note that it is critical for you to qualify your prospects very well before going to see them. Otherwise, you will waste time finding that your prospect is not qualified.

Personally, I do all of my appointments in my office although I would have more appointments if I went to people's homes. Because I have limited time, by scheduling appointments only in my office, I meet with only the most qualified and motivated people.

In our company, here's how we implement a direct-response advertising system. We mail an emotionally compelling piece that offers a free booklet. We then follow up, call after six to eight days, qualify the respondent, and offer an appointment if the respondent is qualified. We call only those who responded to the mail and requested the booklet.

As mentioned previously, we get fewer appointments because we do not go to anyone's home. Yet we have a much higher closing ratio because we are dealing with people who make the time to come to our office and who have some trust in us once we have built our credibility as experts by sending our booklet. We make fewer but higher-quality and larger sales. For example, our average annuity sale using this method averages over $150,000.

In a later section on long-term care, I will tell you how one megaproducer uses direct mail to sell over four hundred long-term care policies per year.

Seminars

If you've developed the opinion that seminars don't work for building your business, you're right—in a way. Seminars don't work when they are done incorrectly. But make a few changes, and you can have sixty to seventy people attending every month to hear your wisdom.

First, just as with advertising headlines, you must promise something your audience actually wants. You won't have winning seminars with titles like these.

POOR SEMINAR TITLES

- What's Happening in the Stock Market
- Investing for the New Millennium
- How to Select Mutual Funds
- Come Hear Our Chief Economist Joe Guesswork
- Three Items Every Senior Must Know
- What to Expect from Stocks in the Coming Year

Not only do these titles have me sleeping before my head hits the pillow, but they also lack any emotional pull. These are seminars that attract eight people. You could increase your attendance fourfold with the right title, such as, "Six Ways Retirees Ruin Their Finances."[31] This title addresses their fear directly and will pull in attendance. (I have very successfully tested this title dozens of times.)

Second, as with direct mail, a good seminar invitation will have several bullet points to pique subsidiary interests and submotivators.

Third, the invitation must show why people should come to hear you. I highly recommend that a printed invitation contain your picture and biography. Without your picture, the invitation is sterile, impersonal, and lacks personality and human touch. The biography tells people why you're special. You may be thinking, "But I've been in the business only two years and have nothing to say about my accomplishments!" I assert that you can write a compelling biography anyway.

Many producers get hung up believing that a good biography is a function of credentials and accomplishments. In fact, a good biography is a function of how well you can craft the piece and accentuate your positive history. Here's an example of the same fact presented poorly and then

[31] This four-fold increase in attendance is documented. The largest seminar production company in the United States claims that their invitation gets a 0.3 percent response rate. The seminar system my company produces gets a 1.2 percent response rate.

presented in its best light:

POOR PRESENTATION

John Jones is a CFP.

BEST LIGHT

John Jones is a well-known financial educator in Philadelphia and a Certified Financial Planner (CFP). To become a Certified Financial Planner, John pursued two years of course work, passed five rigorous tests, and then a comprehensive, two-day, ten-hour exam, proving his expertise in the areas of taxes, investments, asset protection, and estate planning.

CFP® and CERTIFIED FINANCIAL PLANNER® are federally registered marks of the Certified Financial Planner Board of Standards, Inc.

Which of the above speakers would you want to hear? (Later, in the section on getting your name in the press, you will find sample biographies to use on a seminar invitation or whenever you are presenting yourself to the public.)

Understand that your seminar must be designed around your audience's habits and time schedule. You will lose senior attendees if you schedule your seminar after 7 P.M. in the winter because many seniors do not like to go out after dark. Some seniors have trouble seeing well and avoid driving in the dark. Macular degeneration is exclusively an age-related vision problem. Single women (many of whom are widows) may also avoid going out at night. It is a simple matter to honor your prospects' time schedules and habits, yet many producers ignore it and fail at seminars. In such cases, the principal problem is failure to really know the target audience.

Honor your audience's habits and preferences rather than your own. Seniors (retirees) generally rise early in the morning and schedule golf, tennis, shopping, doctor appointments, dentist appointments, and meetings with the accountant or attorney on weekday mornings. Therefore, never hold a seminar on a weekday morning because you would be competing with a lot of other activity in your prospects' schedules. Schedule seminars either for Saturday mornings (when the doctor, dentist, accountant, and attorney are closed and any senior knows better than to schedule golf and tennis on Saturday morning—the most crowded time) or weekday afternoons at 3:30 P.M.

Select a seminar location that is well known, convenient, and in neutral territory. Some financial professionals attempt to hold seminars in their office buildings. Bad idea. This is not neutral territory, and some prospective attendees will not come for fear of being trapped in a high-pressure sales situation. Think about buying a car—whose turf are you on? Is it comfortable for you?

Therefore, never use your office as a seminar location. Rather, use a local restaurant that has existed for more than twenty years—a place everyone in town knows and likes. It's familiar, neutral, and convenient. The best place is where the seniors like to eat. You do not need to feed your audience just because you use a restaurant for your location. Many restaurants are happy to rent an extra room or even open for your seminar at a time when they are normally closed.

What about hotels? Some people perceive them as a place for transients and may associate you with the snake-oil salesman who is here today, gone tomorrow. In addition, some hotels have conference rooms in a location that requires people to negotiate a maze of hallways. Do you want your prospects to enter your seminar frustrated? Hold a seminar in a hotel only if you can't do it in a restaurant.

A country club location can send the wrong signal, too. Some people could feel intimidated that the seminar must be for the "upper crust," and some may even misinterpret that the seminar is for club members or golfers. Picture your perfect prospect—a retired plumber who lives in a middle-income neighborhood with a $3 million net worth. He's right out of *The Millionaire Next Door* (by Thomas Stanley and William Danko). He is never contacted by financial professionals, and he has his money in CDs and fixed annuities. This guy's favorite shirt has a tear in the pocket. Would he be comfortable coming to the country club? Of course, if you are targeting an exclusively upper-class audience, then a country club is fine.

What about community centers or schools? When sophisticated investors (or so they think) get your invitation and see that your seminar will be held at the local adult school, do you know what they think? "This event at the school must be introductory in nature and not of interest to me, an experienced investor." Public facilities are best used when you are targeting a less experienced and less affluent audience.

How to Invite Seniors to a Seminar

There are three ways you can invite people to a seminar: using telemarketers, direct mail, and newspaper advertising. Following are the pros and cons of each.

Using telemarketers consumes a lot of your time in hiring, training, and firing. If you have them work in your office rather than hiring a service, you will also need some office space and additional phones. For each hour of work, you can expect one caller to obtain one attendee who will actually show up. (Three prospects will say they will attend, but your fallout rate will be 50 to 70 percent.) I've paid callers $5 per hour, plus $5 per buying unit who attended. The best aspect of using telemarketers is the low cost; the worst aspect is the time you must commit to managing them. What's more, the quality of prospect who responds to a phone invitation is typically the worst. Often, these are weak prospects who must be convinced to attend.

Newspaper advertising is far too expensive and ineffective in most metropolitan areas. (I have never gotten a good return from newspaper ads.) However, inserts (the newspaper will insert your 8.5" x 11" flyer into the fold of the newspaper) are inexpensive and effective. You can focus your insert distribution on selected Zip codes. Typically, for every ten thousand inserts, eighteen buying units (a buying unit is either an individual or a couple) attend my seminar. I spend a total of $500, which yields a cost per attendee of $27. The negative aspect of inserts is that you may have unqualified attendees since you cannot prequalify people. As a result, you may find yourself in an appointment after a seminar with someone whose greatest concern is what to do with a maturing $5,000 CD.

Direct mail is by far the most effective method to use in metropolitan areas. The cost per attendee is the highest, but the quality of attendees is also the highest, which results in your seminar producing more business and gaining the greatest profits. By sending three thousand invitations to a highly targeted audience, you'll get about thirty-five buying units to attend—a cost of $40 per buying unit. I highly recommend using this more expensive method because it produces the best end results: more qualified new clients who have money to invest.

Many of the techniques that work best and attract the largest audience are counterintuitive. For example, some would think that you maximize your seminar attendance by giving attendees plenty of advance notice. In fact, your attendance will double if you send the invitation only eight to nine days in advance of your seminar. My intuition about why this is so: If you send the invitation early, the interested recipients put it aside, knowing they have plenty of time to respond. And even with every intention to attend, they bury that invitation under other mail or other concerns. By sending the invitation only eight to nine days in advance, you force the interested recipient to respond right away because your event is next week. Your invitation demands an urgent response.

What about providing food? Some producers and seminar marketing companies will tell you that it's essential to feed attendees to fill up the room. In fact, it's not necessary, and based on all the data we have analyzed, it will increase your costs and not necessarily increase your results. Food draws attendance in an attempt to compensate for a weak invitation system—and it attracts eaters rather than serious investors.

One seminar mailing company (which insists that you feed attendees) mails five thousand invitations and gets sixty buying units (about 110 people) to a seminar. Your cost is $3,250 for the mailing, and then you need to feed 110 people at a cost of approximately $15 each—an additional $1,650. You spend $4,900 and expect to receive appointments with 30 percent of the buying units—about eighteen appointments. Your cost per appointment is $272.

At my seminars, I do not feed people (light refreshments are provided, never a meal). I send three thousand invitations and get thirty-five buying units (about sixty people) to attend. I get appointments with 65 percent—more than twenty buying units. Cost per appointment is $75. While it's true that I get fewer attendees because I do not feed people a meal, I get a higher percentage of appointments, and my cost per attendee and cost per appointment is lower.

How to Turn Attendees into Appointments

As the seminar draws to a close, announce that you need a small favor from the attendees: "Please complete the evaluation forms you received at the beginning of the seminar and," you continue without taking a breath, "the evaluation form is also your lottery ticket today."[32]

Let's face it, most people could care less about filling out evaluation forms, so you should give them a reason to do so. Make it so they can win something by completing and returning the form.

On the form, ask some specific questions about your attendees' experience before you offer them the opportunity for the appointment with you. Never ask for an appointment; rather, give them the opportunity to request an appointment. This may seem like semantics, but this approach is far more powerful. With the right wording, you will be in a more appealing position when they request the appointment of you, rather than you requesting (begging for) an appointment with them. People who request an appointment keep it.

WHAT TO SAY

"Folks, let's recap what you learned today . . .

"You learned three ways to increase your income by thirty percent or more. You learned the two essential factors to make money in the stock market. You learned the most important issue for protecting the assets you've worked so hard to accumulate.

[32] You can get a copy of my evaluation form at *www.nfcom.com/items.htm.*

"All of this will assist you in making more profit and protecting your financial future.

"Now I need a small favor from you. I need some feedback on how I did today. Please open your packets. Inside, you will find a seminar evaluation like this."

You show the evaluation form on the overhead.

"This form will also be your lottery ticket today. Someone will walk out today the big winner. Please take a minute and give me some feedback. I will then collect these forms. Who needs a pen?" (Have an assistant rush over to deliver a pen.) "We are also going to have a quick drawing for a prize so you can have something of immediate value to take with you, and these forms will be your lottery tickets.

"How many of you like to go on cruises?"

Hands will go up, and they will say, "Yeah!"

"That's great—I didn't say I was giving away a cruise today, I just wanted to know if you like cruises." They'll laugh.

"Notice that the odds in this lottery are much better than the state lottery. So please take a minute and complete the evaluation form."

I walk the attendees through each step of the evaluation. *This is the most important part of the seminar*. It's where you close appointments. Read the items, and then wait as they fill in the first two questions on the form. Then continue when they get to the middle of the form:

"By the way, you will notice that on the middle half of the form, you can check off if you would like to meet with me individually. I am happy to spend an hour with anyone who was here today and give you some individual advice. My normal rate is one-hundred-fifty dollars per hour, but I have set aside free hours for those of you here today.

"I hope no one is disappointed, but if you take advantage of the free hour meeting, *I am NOT going to sell you anything.* That's not what the meeting is for. When we meet, you bring your tax return and investment statements. I'll review those with you, and you'll have an opportunity to ask any questions you have. In fact, please write down your questions and concerns and bring them with you to the meeting. I'll give you reports on your investments showing you exactly how they are doing, and I promise to show you at least one significant error you are making with your money that you're not even aware of. So please check off this box if you'd like to avoid unnecessary mistakes."

You point on the overhead to the box where they can commit to an appointment time. "Select the time and day that's best for you. If you're not sure, make your best guess, because we will call you tomorrow to confirm that this time is good for you."

Put the final overhead on the projector, which should be a profile of your premium clients, and say, "These people are the types of people who get value from the appointment.

"If you are unhappy with your investment performance or don't even know what it is.

"If you own annuities that have dropped in rate . . . "

Read through the profile on your overhead. The purpose of this extra step is to help people identify if they would benefit from the appointment with you. This may seem simple, but it is my experience that people need to be led by the hand. If they see an item that pertains to them on the overhead, they will think, *That's me. I guess I should sign up for the appointment.* I am certain that this last overhead has helped me gain another one or two appointments per seminar.

As people finish the evaluations, have your lottery. Ask attendees to please pass their forms to the back of the room, and have your assistant pick up the forms.

Then hold the lottery: Take all of the evaluations and place them face down, then mix them up on the table, and pick one. Give away something meaningful to this audience. (I give away copies of my book, *Retirement Investing,* which you can purchase with your picture and name imprinted as explained in the appendix.)

Thank the participants and let them know that you are looking forward to helping them in the future.

That's it. You spend ninety minutes giving a motivational presentation, and you walk out with twenty appointments *in your office* over the next two weeks.

Attendees sign up for the appointment because you promise two things: 1) You will make no attempt to sell them anything at that appointment, and 2) You will show them at least one significant financial mistake they are making and are not even aware of.

As a result, you can ask for and get 100 percent of the people who have scheduled an appointment to bring in their lists of investments and tax returns.

Do you think you could do business with someone who comes to your office with a list of investments and tax return and wants to hear what you have to say? This method of doing seminars and closing appointments right at the seminar is so successful that I can't imagine why any professional would ever make cold calls! In the next chapter, you'll learn what to do when prospects come for the appointment.

It's essential that you close appointments right at the seminar. What I am about to explain is worth ten thousand times the cost of this book for producers who give seminars: *Never let attendees leave the seminar without a firm appointment.* Many seminar presenters ignore this simple advice. They provide a great presentation and then spend the two days after the seminar on the phone with attendees, "begging" for appointments.

Checking a box on a card that says, "Call me, I would like to meet," is not a commitment to an appointment. This puts you back in the position of the pursuer. You will never appear as a professional when you keep calling just to get an appointment.

How can you get them to schedule a firm appointment at the seminar? Invite the attendees to do so, and then tell them to select a time and day from those listed on your evaluation form.

Generate an Abundance of Prospects

Many financial advisors are in the mode of chasing prospects. Some financial advisors have closed their doors to new prospects because they do not have the time to take on more clients. In which camp would you rather be?

Some producers think that qualified prospects are scarce. In fact, you've been taught to think this way in your sales training:

BOGUS SALES TRAINING

- "The sale starts when the prospect says no."
- "It takes six contacts before you can expect to make a sale."
- "You've got to find out the real objection before you can close."

These "principles" make selling difficult, waste your time, and give any sales profession a bad name. In fact, this ineffective paradigm of selling, which often hides under the guise of admirable persistence, is based on a false premise. Most likely, you have lived your entire career with an assumption that qualified prospects are scarce. It may be hard to see that you live with this notion. But if you've gone back again and again to the same prospects after they have said no many times, you have been gripped by the false notion that qualified prospects are scarce. Isn't it true that if you believed good prospects were plentiful, you would have just moved on to the next prospect and not wasted your time?

But you've been taught to be persistent (*obnoxious* from the prospect's perspective) and you believe such persistence is a good thing! Doesn't this make you weary? And isn't it a huge waste of your time?

So you've gotten tired of selling, you believe that prospects are difficult, you've even sacrificed your integrity at times because you just wanted to make a sale even if someone was only marginally inclined to do business. You went home tired at the end of the day.

It doesn't need to be this way, and professional, successful financial services salespeople do not do business this way. They have one very different belief. *They believe qualified prospects are abundant!*

Please think a minute about some big producers you know. Don't they act like everyone is a good prospect? And doesn't the universe make their belief come true by continuing to deliver high-quality prospects to them? It may seem they have the magic touch, but it's not magic. These successful producers simply have a belief that's consistent with reality. Good prospects are all over the place!

So the successful producer does not grind on a prospect or return with the same story. Sure, they may ask prospects why they say no. But they do this only to be sure that their own communication has been complete and that they have understood all of the prospects' concerns. When they see clearly that a prospect is not interested, they shake hands and say good-bye.

If you want to reach higher levels of production and enjoy your work more, just move on when you do not have an interested prospect. Better yet, make sure that your prospecting system generates appointments only with interested and qualified people.

Obtain Business from Your Peers

I see too many financial professionals grovel for business. They call the same prospect back a number of times; they study closing techniques, attend motivational seminars, and buy motivational tapes. They attend seminars to learn how to get more referrals from their clients. All this activity to get more clients. Does your doctor do this? Does your CPA do this to get more clients?

So why don't the other professions work so hard to get more clients? Here's the Zen paradox—they get more clients because they are less covetous of clients. Let me explain.

It's my experience that average retail financial professionals try to hold onto every piece of business. Instead of introducing a client to a long-term care expert when that's what the client wants, they attempt to learn what they can about long-term care, make a half-baked presentation, and don't get the sale.

Notice that doctors and attorneys do not practice the same behavior. They refer business like crazy to each other. They realize that some people specialize in particular areas and they send the business to their peers. For example, when you have a serious ear infection, your general practitioner will send you to an ear, nose, and throat specialist. Fortunately, doctors draw the line on their knowledge and do not attempt to exceed their expertise. Similarly, a business attorney will refer you to an estate planning attorney to have a trust prepared.

Financial professionals, however, are often shortsighted, want to keep all the business for themselves, and rarely refer business to a peer. In other words, people in financial services are plagued by a scarcity mentality.

The scarcity mentality makes them afraid that they do not know where the next business will come from, so they need to do all the business with a client in hand. Then financial producers subscribe to edicts such as the following.

MORE BOGUS SALES ADVICE

- "Don't leave until you are told no six times."
- "Be persistent."
- "Try the alternate choice close."

Until we cease the scarcity mentality and stop these sales tactics, the public will not consider stockbrokers and insurance agents professionals. Financial producers do *not* share the same public stature as doctors and attorneys, and will not until they start treating their peers as colleagues rather than competitors.

So what can you do? Get into relationships with other professionals whose expertise complements your own. Next time you think about referrals, don't seek them from your clients, give them and seek them from your peers.

Prospecting Systems

Here's a comparison of two prospecting systems. One produces good quality prospects, the other produces people who make you tired.

When you cold call for appointments, you generate low-quality prospects because, in many instances, you have to convince the prospect to see you. Is it any wonder that 30 percent of the prospect appointments you make this way are no-shows or cancellations? In addition, can you see that a lower-quality prospect will succumb to telephone pressure while the better-quality prospect will make the first move? The better-quality prospect will react to direct mail, a recommendation from a friend, an advertisement, or a seminar invitation.

Instead of cold calling, what would happen if you placed an advertisement offering a free booklet about a particular topic in which you had expertise? Those people who called from the advertisement for that booklet would be self-motivated. That's the type of prospect you want: people who have initiative and take action.

Do you see the difference in how your prospecting system determines the type of prospects you develop?

Why Some Advisors Chase Prospects

Those advisors who are chasing prospects do so because of one or both of these weaknesses in their practices:

1. inadequate sales skills, and/or
2. inadequate marketing systems as previously described.

Becoming better at selling does not mean convincing more people to buy. Selling is not about convincing. It's about listening, asking appropriate questions, and guiding the prospect to an agreeable recommendation.

These are sophisticated skills, so I continue to be shocked by the number of professionals who must sell themselves but have never taken any formal sales training. Few people have the innate ability to have an effective sales conversation without learning it. Related expertise and experience are helpful, but not sufficient. You need training designed to make you a sales professional—this means you need sales-specific training. Despite graduating from college at nineteen, then earning my

CPA and Harvard MBA, the first thing I realized when entering sales was that I needed sales training fast! And my training never stops.

You can start or improve your training today. Before proceeding, take action on one of the above avenues by ordering the books below or calling the Dale Carnegie office in your area.

THE THREE BEST TOOLS FOR SALES TRAINING

1. The Dale Carnegie Sales Training (presented in most major cities)
2. Neil Rackham's books, *Spin Selling* and the *Spin Selling Handbook*
3. Bill Bachrach's book and tapes, *Values-Based Selling*

Chapter 5 Summary

I could expand this chapter into several books to provide greater detail. However, I have provided concisely the key variables for successful seminars, advertising campaigns, and direct mail marketing systems. These methods generate substantial business, and the key is to test and adjust based on your results. Based on each month's results, I continue to refine the systems I have used in my practice for years.

6 A Model for Selling to Seniors

This chapter will help you do more business when in a sales situation with a senior.

I have provided a discussion of tactical "do's" and "don'ts," as well as a strategy for positioning yourself in the sales conversation.

Seniors want to comparison shop. They know products differ, and they will look for the one most suitable. You might think this attribute makes seniors a tough market to dominate. Not so—you just need to do the comparison shopping for them.

When I meet with a prospect, I make it very clear that I am an independent advisor. I will do the shopping among several different companies (annuity, life, LTC, investment) and find the most suitable choice for them. This allows me to control the client and never get into a product "pissing contest" with another professional. If you are representing the products and services of only one company, however, you will need to present the stability and size of your company so that prospects want to do business with you and your firm.

Just as with your printed material, leave your jargon out of conversations with seniors. If you do not explain opportunities in plain English, you will lose the sale. You must realize that terms in your everyday vocabulary, such as *underwriting, volatility, turnover, 12b-1, load, allocation, adjusted gross income, rating, elimination period, lapse,* and others, are meaningless gobbledygook to your prospect. Remember that these people have been around six decades and more. They won't tolerate being confused and they certainly won't buy from you. They will simply find someone who can explain opportunities in plain English and show them why it's in their emotional best interest to act.

JARGON	ENGLISH
underwriting	health review
volatility	choppiness
turnover	amount of buying and selling
12b-1	annual sales fee
allocation	diversification
adjusted gross income	the total of all your income
elimination period	deductible period
annuitization	monthly payments
death benefit	amount of life insurance

Issue of Control

Seniors like control, and this often translates into a preference for liquidity. Fortunately, most financial investments are liquid, but that point should always be articulated. For example, when presenting a managed investment account, you could say the following:

"Mr. Jones, ABC will be managing your money, but remember, you can shut off this program any day. The stocks and bonds can be sold any time and your assets converted back to cash. I just want you to know that you're always the boss. It's your money."

Although the issue of liquidity in financial instruments seems so obvious to us in the financial arena, the idea of handing money over to a professional money manager can feel like a loss of control to the prospect. It can remain an unstated objection that leaves you wondering why you did not get the business.

Issue of Independence

Seniors don't want to be a burden on anyone or lose the ability to function and take care of themselves. Yet they fear this day may not be far off. Calming this fear will provide you business.

WHAT TO SAY TO CALM FEARS OF DEPENDENCE

1. "This immediate annuity will provide a continuous monthly income, ensuring that you will always have this income to maintain your lifestyle."
2. "This long-term care policy will provide the funds for you to take care of yourself so that you are never a burden on your spouse or your children."
3. "Mr. Jones, if you pass away, do you realize that your pension stops, and this will cut your household income by two-thirds? Do you see how this will create a hardship for your wife? This $250,000 life policy will eliminate that hardship and save her from being dependent on the kids."
4. "Have you noticed that the cost of living keeps rising? Where have you noticed it most? Does this concern you for the future? That's exactly why I'm recommending this conservative growth fund. It has excellent potential to keep up with living costs, so that you will remain financially independent and will have enough to take care of yourself."

Seniors Are Skeptical

Once you've lived for six or seven decades, it's natural to feel you've seen it all, and you may be a little cautious about any new proposition. Take this into account when making initial contact with seniors.

Cold calling is a tough way to prospect seniors. They are told repeatedly by the media about rip-off scams perpetuated on the telephone. Skepticism runs high. Therefore, you need to prove yourself. I recommend not using cold calling to seniors for a few reasons.

Why Not to Cold-Call Seniors

1. You are a total stranger on the phone and senior skepticism will run the highest with this form of initial contact.
2. Some seniors have a hearing problem, which makes telephone contact more difficult.
3. An increasing number of states have statutes limiting hours and forms of cold calling.

However, if you must cold call, an initial contact should be followed with some literature that same day. And that information should contain your picture and your biography—work history, where you're from, where you went to school, where you reside (neighborhood), and how many kids you have. Scam artists never provide this information, so this type of written communication will go a long way toward defusing skepticism. In addition, you become a person rather than just a voice on the phone.

Sending literature to seniors is important. First, they like to read, and an item in writing allows them to review it, think about it, and jot down questions. They can move sequentially through the piece, point by point, and they can take it at their own pace. For many seniors, reading is much easier than quickly thinking of the right questions to ask on a telephone call.

Repetition of contact is important. After the first piece of mail, you should have some follow-up pieces that get mailed every ten days. Contact your prospects four days after each piece is mailed, and give them the opportunity to set an appointment.

If you have identified a good prospect but still do not have the appointment, then use long-term repetition. A monthly newsletter is a superior way to enforce that you have staying power and that you are a constant in an ever-changing world. Such repetitive contact breeds comfort. Your future contact will be a warm call.

The Face-to-Face Sale

Let's assume you have made an appointment with your senior prospect, either through cold calling or through a response to an ad, a seminar, or direct mail response. The following presents three ways to position yourself with the prospect. The diagrams show a literal position at the table, but I am addressing the figurative position of how you relate to the prospect.

The Win-Lose Sales Model

The "old" model of selling pitted the salesperson as an adversary against the customer. We envision the salesperson sitting on one side of the desk with the prospect on the other side. (We'll use the positions of the chairs as a metaphor to describe three selling models in this section.) The dynamic was, "I win, you lose."

The advisor (really a salesperson) in this scenario adheres to these precepts:

- "I'm gonna sell this guy."
- "Let's see how I can make the biggest commission."
- "I'll show her why my product is best."
- "I need to talk him up from a $50,000 commitment to $150,000."

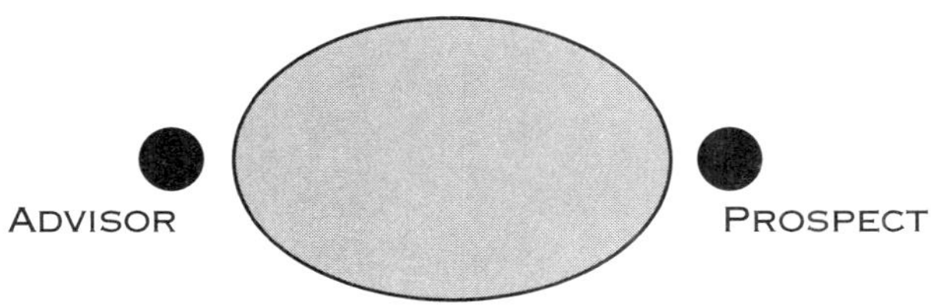

Although this model is outmoded, it still exists in virtually every aspect of financial sales. It's the approach still used widely by people selling financial products and living trusts in prospects' homes, and it works with people who . . .

- don't have much investing experience,
- make small dollar commitments (under $25,000), and
- are among the lower socioeconomic half of seniors who are accustomed to purchasing "goods" (e.g., financial products) vs. "services" (e.g., money management).

The Consultative Sales Model

The clients you really want to cultivate, the more affluent top half of the senior market, won't be interested in what you have to offer them if you use this old model. The current model, that of consultative selling, won't work with the right seniors either. In this scenario, the advisor sits on the same side of the desk as the client.

- "I'll teach the client why she needs more stock in her portfolio."
- "When we're done, he'll understand why (asset allocation, universal life, load funds) are the best way to go."
- "Let me show her this chart of stock performance from 1926, and then she'll see . . ."
- "When he sees how much estate tax is involved, then he'll want this . . ."

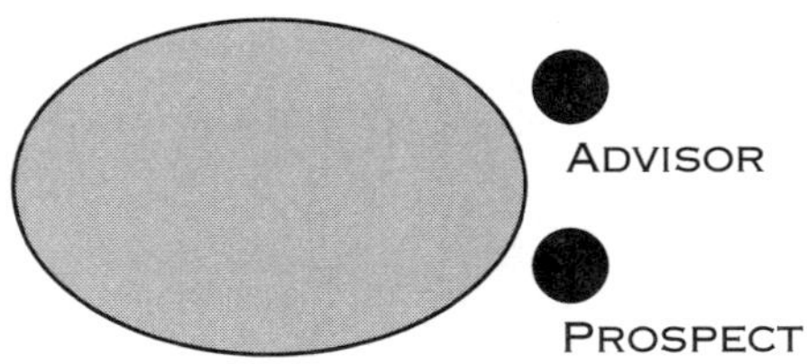

This type of approach, in which the salesperson becomes the educator and seemingly the trusted advisor, will mostly fail. This approach generates a lot of "I'll think about it" from prospects you will never see again.

Why? Because many seniors are not interested in learning why they should do something. They don't understand it, they are not in your business and not familiar with the basics (which are often assumed in most sales presentations), and they quickly grow tired of a lesson in investment fundamentals. Moreover, a lifetime of experience has wedded them to their opinions.

Remember the "sample of one" and the two financial planners who presented an equipment-leasing program to a retired investor. Quite frankly, the program made a lot of sense given this investor's needs and financial circumstances. Within the first few minutes, he replied, "My neighbor is in the equipment leasing business, and he says it's risky." Too bad these advisors didn't understand the power of the sample of one; they continued to educate the prospect about how leasing really worked and how the risk was removed in their program. What a waste of time! This senior's experience (what his neighbor told him) spoke louder than any logic or set of facts. These well-trained financial planners had little knowledge about senior mentality.

The Therapist Model

The model that works with affluent seniors (those able to invest $100,000 or more) is the "therapist model." In this scenario, the advisor does not sit across from the prospect or together with the prospect, but at a ninety-degree angle.

- The therapist does not sit on the couch.
- The therapist wants to figure out what motivates the other person.
- The therapist wants to know what "rules" or biases the client has, just as the advisor uncovers likes and dislikes, regardless of validity.
- The therapist is thinking, *Where can I achieve a balance of what's right and what this client will accept?*
- The therapist is also trying to find the territories of common ground with the client.

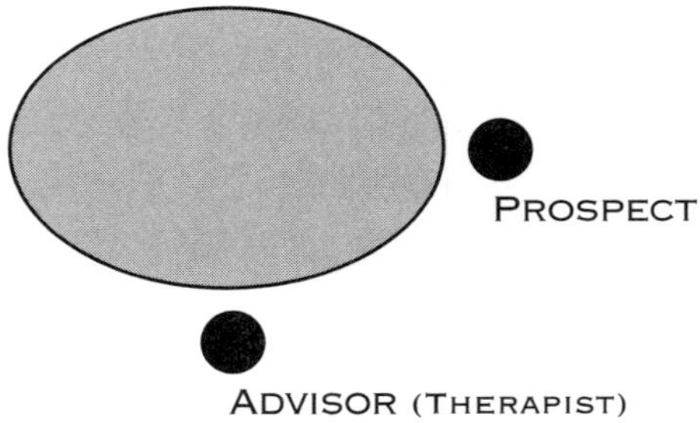

In other words, the therapist advisor wants to find the middle ground of what will satisfy the prospect and what the advisor can offer. The idea of doing "what's best" for the prospect is the road to nowhere, because the advisor typically defines "what's best" as some technical solution that is based on college classes, study for credentials, and hours of continuing education. These technical solutions are not what are best, because if the prospect leaves without any commitment, there's no business and the prospect is no better off. Therefore, the goal is to identify what solution will improve the prospect's financial situation and be emotionally and psychologically acceptable to the prospect.

In this model, the advisor is friend and adversary. Like the therapist, he or she wants to help prospects but isn't going to let them get away with any nonsense either. The advisor's job, like the therapist's, is to make a difference. And in the arena of finances, making a difference means having the prospect turn money over to the advisor.

To return to the example of the planners presenting the equipment leasing idea, they would have been smart to drop it immediately upon hearing the prospect's opinion formed by his neighbor's comment. The time would have been better spent asking the prospect why he owned the investments he did, which investments had been his best successes, and which had been failures. The advisors would have had a much better map of the direction to proceed by capitalizing on what the investor was already favorably disposed to.

Some readers may think my advice is harsh. How irresponsible I must be to suggest that you do anything other than the very best for the prospect! In fact, I am suggesting what is very best, which is getting the prospect to take action. What's technically "very best" may be the farthest point away from your prospect's comfort level.

To be at either end of the spectrum—offering only what your client will like or only what you believe is best technically—is irresponsible. The inexperienced advisor going for the "right" solution will lose the prospect, and there will be no business. The unrelenting "closer" will sell anything the prospect agrees to (e.g., the prospect has 100 percent of the portfolio in municipal bonds, and the advisor recommends more municipal bonds). I assert that the best solution, somewhere in the middle, produces action by the prospect.

Here's another look at the three sales approaches:

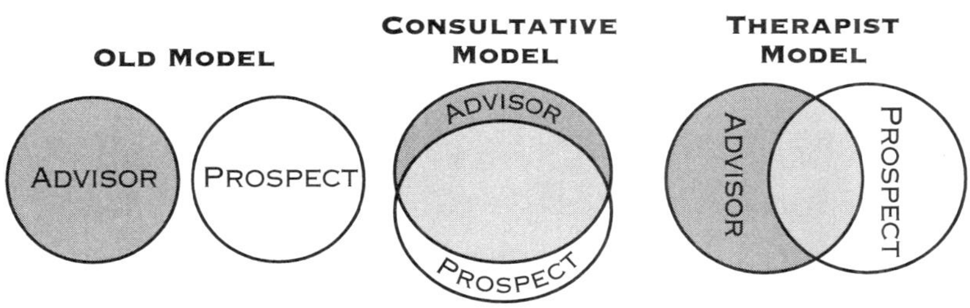

In the old model, there is no overlap between the interests of the advisor and prospect. In the consultative model, the advisor attempts to show the prospect the "right" thing to do. Like the consultant, whether the plan ultimately gets implemented is secondary (most consultants get paid for the consulting, not on the implementation). In the therapist model, the advisor and prospect have overlapping objectives, but the advisor is most focused on the prospect taking some action that will improve the prospect's financial situation.

It's a misnomer that a number of large securities firms have titled their financial advisors "financial consultants." A consultant takes a fee for advice. The consultant's compensation is not dependent upon the client following the advice. Consultants are paid for an intellectual product, and their duty is to tell their clients the technically best action to take.

In fact, financially successful financial advisors are not acting as consultants. They are either using the old model, the adversary model, selling lots of product and then moving on to the next prospect (i.e., smile and dial), or they are using the therapist model and balancing the right advice with the client's emotional biases. These advisors are developing clients, not merely customers.

The therapist paradigm is most successful with the affluent senior.

The First Appointment

Have prospects bring copies of their tax returns and their lists of investments. Tell them to bring these items at the close of a seminar, and you'll get 100 percent compliance. Also tell them it will be a one-hour appointment.

By placing a time boundary on the appointment, you secure three benefits:

1. The prospect understands that your time is limited. Your stature is enhanced.
2. Rather than spending their time telling you stories, they will get down to business because the time is limited.
3. If the discussion is incomplete at the end of an hour, it provides the obvious need to schedule another appointment.

What to do once the prospects arrive? The structure of my first appointment is as follows.

WHAT TO DO

- **FIRST TEN MINUTES.** Schmoozing, smiling, rapport building: *How long have you lived in the area? Do your children live nearby? You have great tans, are you golfers?*

- **NEXT FORTY-FIVE MINUTES.** Get down to business and provide a brief explanation without jargon to explain services. Then turn to fact finding:
    - Cover questions and concerns.
    - Conduct fact finding, listening for likes and dislikes.
    - Provide general, non-specific feedback.
- **LAST FIVE MINUTES.** Explain the benefits and estimated financial impact to be delivered (e.g., lower the fees on your investments and save you $3,500 per year, get you on a system for investing, protect your assets from long-term care needs—a potential savings of $250,000, reduce your income tax by $6,000 annually). Before you say goodbye, offer to schedule a follow-up appointment with recommendations on how to achieve the above benefits. Do not sell a financial plan. People do not want a financial plan, they want the benefits of a financial plan. Therefore, use this wording to close:

  "My fee to properly analyze your circumstances and provide recommendations is $xxx. If:
  - saving you $3,500 every year on your investment fees,
  - protecting your assets from long term care needs, a potential savings of $250,000,
  - reducing your income tax by $6,000 annually
  is worth $xxx, then let's meet again next Wednesday."

  If you cannot charge fees for this service, say something like "Mr. and Mrs. Jones, if I can provide all these benefits for you, is there any reason we can't do business?"

Here's the nitty gritty: After you've had some friendly conversation and told prospects about your services, start taking notes on what your prospects have to say. Offer, "So that I make sure we cover any questions or concerns you have in our hour together, let me jot them down so we won't forget." Most every prospect has two or three items they want to discuss, especially if you told them at the seminar to jot down their questions or concerns. It's amazing what people will do when you instruct them.

Then proceed with fact finding. Ask questions so that you can put together an income statement and balance sheet right on the yellow pad in front of you.

Fact Finding

You can begin, "Folks, tell me about your sources of income. Are you receiving any pensions? Social security? Rents? Interest/dividends?" And so on.

"Now let's take a look at your investments." (They have brought in their statements or their balance sheet.) As you look these over, make some unsettling comments, if appropriate, about their investments: "Do you know what you're really earning on these investments? How long have you had them? How did you come to own these investments?" (Our firm provides a program that teaches you the strategies on how to ask the right questions to increase the number of prospects that become clients - see the appendix for more details.)

Although you are asking tactical questions, you should be listening for likes and dislikes, preferences, emotional comfort zones, hopes and desires. For example, they may say, "We've always been a little nervous about stocks, so we have not owned any." This should count heavily in the recommendations you prepare for them. A large element of your recommendations must include a commitment to their comfort (no comfort equals no implementation). Therefore, in this example, you would recommend little if any stock market exposure, in light of the most technically appropriate recommendations that you can make. Then proceed with giving your opinions.

Provide Feedback

"Now," you say, "Let me give you some of my thoughts. You had two concerns you mentioned in the beginning. Since I know more about your circumstances, I can tell you this . . ." Proceed to provide some useful but unspecific direction or advice, then offer, "I can get together some specific recommendations regarding those issues," such as a long-term care quotation, analysis of an annuity, review of their trust, a money management program, etc. "With those specific recommendations, you will have precise answers to your questions.

"In addition, I would like to present you with independent reports on each of your investments so you can really see what's going on. Some of these are fine, but some of these, quite frankly, are clunkers." The prospect typically agrees, saying something like, "We know we should have sold some of these but . . ."

Your response: "Folks, let me propose this. Let's schedule a time to meet next week." Suggest the same day and time. "I want to put together some answers to your questions, and let's review the reports I will get on each of your investments." If you subscribe to *Value Line* and *Morningstar* on CD-ROM, you'll have quick access to the reports you need.

Because I am a Registered Investment Advisor, I always conclude the first meeting with something like the following: "This will take me three hours to put together. My normal rate is one-hundred-fifty dollars per hour, so if you think that four-hundred-fifty dollars would be reasonable to isolate the investments you should sell and what you should do about [their two issues], then let's meet next week."

If they say they want to think about it, that's great! Because I just learned not to spend more time with these folks until they want me to. If $450 is a barrier to proceeding, then I am not the financial advisor for them. Ninety percent of the people want to meet again and ask me, "Should we pay you now?" These are the types of clients you and I want. Using this model, I am never chasing people to make a decision. I work with the people who want to work with me. If you are thinking that I have some luxury of picking my clients that you do not, that's not so. In the previous section, I explained exactly how we generate an abundance of prospects so that we never need to chase anyone or convince them to work with us.

If you cannot charge fees for some reason (e.g., you're not a Registered Investment Advisor), it is more difficult to test a prospect's seriousness. All you can do is ask, "Mr. and Mrs. Jones, when we meet next week, if my recommendations make sense to you and you see that there are ways for you to do better financially, will there be anything that would stop us from doing business together?" I don't like to ask this question as I find it presumptuous, but it will be better for you than spending three hours putting materials together and then finding out some cousin works at ABC Securities!

Use the first appointment to fact find. Be clear that the objective of the first appointment is to schedule a second appointment (assuming you want to work with the prospect). Do not try to close business at the first appointment. This two-session system will result in larger accounts and doing more comprehensive business with clients.

The Second Appointment

Schedule the second appointment one week after the first appointment. The objectives for this appointment are as follows.

What to Do

1. Review the issues discussed the last time and confirm what you heard.
2. Present your recommendations, show how they address the issues from the first appointment, and show the pros and cons of each recommendation. Although some salespeople believe you should present your recommendations in only a positive light, this can raise skepticism. Every intelligent person knows that in the world of investing, there are tradeoffs and risks. So here's my best advice to any financial advisor—you bring up any objection before your prospect does. Fully acknowledge and be willing to discuss the tradeoffs or risks inherent in each recommendation.

3. Advocate moving forward (signing papers) on the recommendations.

Software Tools for Senior Recommendations

We do not present to senior clients a typical "financial plan." The clients you should be seeing will not run out of money during their lifetimes (their resources are sufficient), and they do not need a cash flow budget, nor do you need to regurgitate to them the balance sheet they provided. Therefore, much of the financial planning software I have reviewed, which is geared toward those preparing for retirement, is inappropriate for our retired clients. At my firm, our tools are the following.

- MS Word
- MS Excel
- *Morningstar* (CD-ROM)
- *Value Line* (CD-ROM)

Chapter 6 Summary

The sales process is about psychology, not about explaining the technical details of your favorite recommended mutual fund. It's also about repeating the same process over and over so that you become efficient and effective at helping seniors. Note that you do not need expensive or time-consuming software tools. We spend on average two hours to compile our recommendations, and we average $500,000 of new funds per new client relationship.

We are able to be efficient because the similarity of our clients' needs and desires allows for presentation of the same concepts, products, and services every day. You can replicate this approach.

7 Important Products and Services for the Senior Market

"Matures feel relatively secure, but they are concerned about keeping their share of the pie,"

we are told in the Yankelovich report. "Many worry about outliving their savings or entitlements. Others fear that hard times in their future could turn their financial situation upside down. Matures look for financial products that can help them enhance their standard of living without depleting their savings. Saving is much of what their lives have been about. Don't ask them to give this up. Offer, instead, products that trade some other assets or equity for the income they need today."[33]

Let's look at the products and services that seniors value and how to present them.

Reverse Mortgages

When you read the above quotation, it appears that reverse mortgages should be the hottest product since social security checks. In fact, the sale of reverse mortgages has been dismal. In the three decades in which reverse mortgages have been offered, fewer than 200,000 have been consummated, yet we have 32 million people in the United States aged sixty-five and older.[34]

In fact, in 1996, the Federal Department of Housing and Urban Development (HUD) expanded their insurance of reverse mortgages,

---

[33] Smith and Clurman, *Rocking the Ages.*

[34] National Center for Home Equity Conversion, *www.reverse.org*, 11/3/99.

which removes any risk from the lender. At that time, only 125 of 10,000 eligible Federal Housing Authority (FHA) lenders were making reverse mortgages. HUD blamed this on the fact that they had capped the number of mortgages to insure at 50,000; however, by 1996 only 16,000 mortgages had been issued under the HUD guarantee.[35] Clearly, the FHA's insurance cap was not the reason for slow "sales" of reverse mortgages.

And there is no shortage of potential demand for this product from seniors. Twelve million seniors are eligible for the FHA-insured mortgages, and a study by Cornell University estimated that over 620,000 poor elderly homeowners could raise their incomes above the poverty level with reverse mortgages.[36]

A Few Reasons Seniors Need to Tap Home Equity

- Supplement retirement income
- Make house repairs
- Pay off an existing mortgage and cease monthly payments
- Enhance enjoyment of life—trips, furnishings, a new car
- Take advantage of investment opportunities
- Help relatives, including grandchildren
- Pay for a spouse in a nursing home, get in-home care, or obtain long-term care insurance

Then why, with such large potential demand from seniors and the federal government removing the risk to lenders by insuring the mortgages, have so few loans been made?

Like so many of the impediments to selling financial services to seniors, the *communication* regarding reverse mortgages has been terrible.

[35] "HUD Proposes Major Expansion of Reverse Mortgage Program to Help More Senior Citizen Homeowners," HUD Bulletin No. 96-129, *www.hud.gov/reverspr.html.*

[36] Ibid.

Poor Communication Leads to Poor Sales

The same people selling home mortgages to baby boomers try to sell reverse mortgages to seniors. The problem is that boomers and seniors are so totally different. Boomers are interested in minimizing the monthly payment and getting the lowest interest rates. Seniors are far less interested in the figures and want to know that their security is protected, that no one can take their homes away, that their children will indeed receive any remaining equity after the reverse mortgage is paid. The salesperson is simply not prepared for this conversation. I do not mean they do not have the answers. I mean that they cannot anticipate the questions and provide the right answers (the right answer is often to an unspoken question) because they do not know what to listen for in this market.

In other words, they have the answers to the senior's questions (the content) but they miss the senior's true emotional concerns (the context). The mortgage broker's forty-year-old borrowers have logically/financially oriented content for their questions. ("What's the APR, the monthly payment, the cap?" etc.) Seniors want to know they will not be making a mistake and they will not lose their independence. It's a completely different conversation, even though seniors' questions may *sound similar* to those asked by forty-year-olds.

What's more, the reverse mortgage is being sold as an encumbrance, and seniors do not like the idea of being in debt or having liens. Why did the industry call these *reverse mortgages* rather than *home equity annuities*? It's because banks and financial institutions, which have a product-driven mentality, view reverse mortgages as another debt offering. In fact, if banks were market driven and did the necessary work to understand the customer, this product would not be called a *mortgage,* nor would it be positioned for the homeowner as taking on a liability. Instead, the message could be the following.

A Better Way to Position Home Equity Annuities (a.k.a. Reverse Mortgages)

"You've worked hard. Your generation kept this country safe by fighting two world wars, and you've enjoyed a good economy with increasing house values. Now let that hard work pay dividends back to you with a home equity annuity. Let your home pay you a monthly dividend so you can enjoy life more. Use your dividends to fix up the house, take a trip, or simply buy the grandchildren what they want for Christmas."

A simple change in the name of the instrument, an alteration of the context for the conversation, and the reverse mortgage market is ready to explode overnight. This presents a major opportunity not only for financial institutions in this marketplace, but also for the economy as a whole if trillions of dollars of home equity get pumped into the marketplace.

Estate Planning

Estate planning is an obvious and lucrative service to provide to seniors. In fact, the market for estate planning is pretty thin for any prospect younger than age sixty. I have not met many young or middle-aged people with the foresight to plan their estates. Until someone feels mortality approaching, his or her motivation to do estate planing is slight.

Realize that the market for this service is small—maybe 4 percent of the U.S. population—because there are few estates subject to the estate tax. Sure, everyone needs a will or trust and durable powers, living wills, and so on, but as a financial professional, there's no financial opportunity for you in these documents. Document drafting is the domain of attorneys, and to get involved in this exposes you to legal liability that is not worth it. Your money is to be earned through the sale of insurance products. Unless your prospect's estate exceeds the estate taxable limits ($1,000,000 in the year 2002and 2003), then there is little opportunity for revenue.

Why Much Estate Planning Fails

Financial advisors and attorneys have poorly educated prospects about estate planning and may be poorly educated themselves. The reason many prospects will delay and never do any estate planning is that they perceive reduction of estate taxes is accomplished by giving up ownership of assets, and people resist giving up ownership. For example, assets must be transferred out of an estate into an irrevocable trust, charitable remainder trust (CRT), or someplace where ownership must be relinquished. Unfortunately, prospects equate ownership with control—unless we teach them otherwise.

To remove assets from the estate, the prospect does give up ownership, but need not give up control. The heads of many Fortune 500 companies do not own much of the company, yet they control the corporate plane, the chauffeur-driven limousine, the company ski lodge in Vail, and the $150,000 golf club membership. They may own none of it but can control it and enjoy it. That's what estate planning is about—control without ownership.

Any decent attorney can draft an irrevocable trust that allows your client to access cash in the trust if needed. (A properly drafted irrevocable trust can permit borrowing by the grantor, distributions to the grantor's spouse and family, and power of a special trustee to terminate the trust and return trust assets to the grantor.) And in the case of a CRT, isn't it true that your client gets the income stream and has the power to select and change investments, and only 10 percent of the present value of the gift need go to charity? Isn't that quite a bit of control? And in the case of gifting, can't your prospect place restrictions on the gifts (or make it such that any future gifts will cease if the children don't follow the program)? The point is that we have not educated people about the distinction between ownership and control. It's the perfect estate death—own nothing, control everything.

ESTATE PLANNING BENEFITS FOR THE SENIOR

Once you identify a candidate, there is weak motivation to proceed based solely on saving estate taxes. People want to know what's in it for them. And if you show them how to save estate taxes for the kids, there's nothing in it for them. In my experience, there are few people who want to part with their cash to save their kids a future, intangible tax. So you will need to show how they get a personal benefit.

1. **INCOME TAX SAVINGS.** For example, if your prospect has been wanting to sell an apartment building because he doesn't want to manage tenants, then a CRT or gift annuity would provide a benefit to the prospect. Of course, then the life insurance sale (the wealth replacement trust), which completes the picture for the client, provides your compensation. Additionally, the funds in the CRT create a pool of capital to be managed and an opportunity for management fees.
2. **FULFILLMENT OF A STRONG EMOTIONAL NEED.** Find out about your prospects' relationship with their grandchildren. Often, there is a huge motivation to provide for the grandchildren, a motivation much stronger than providing for their children. I have met many parents who have the attitude, "I had to work for it, my kids can, too." But when it comes to their grandchildren, they want to give as much as possible.

   The approach here is first to establish the desire for the gift. Show how giving $30,000 annually into a trust for the grandkids is a wise thing to do and how the grandchildren will be well provided for, courtesy of their grandparents. Get the trust established and the prospect writing out the checks. At some point, the client will ask, "How should we invest this money for them?"

   "Would you like to know the best way, Mr. Jones? We should invest the money in a variable life insurance policy to provide the largest benefit to your grandchildren."

You have made the sale easier because you have first gotten the gift money segregated. What to do with the gift becomes an easy sale as the client is looking for guidance. (Too many advisors do this backwards. They put the focus on the life policy or the management of the assets rather than first getting the client to segregate the funds to be gifted.)

3. **CHARITABLE INTENT.** Sometimes, the emotional desire will be in the form of charitable intent. But this intent is rare. Americans are not generous with our money, as we give only 1 percent of our incomes to charity. So do not even propose a charitable gift unless your fact finding reveals a predisposition to give. In fact, saying the word "charity" or "charitable" can often cause the end of any estate planning conversation for your prospect. I will tell you more about presenting charitable ideas in a more palatable manner later in this chapter.
4. **DISDAIN FOR THE PAYMENT OF TAXES.** There are a few individuals who have such a disdain for taxes that they are willing to take money out of their pocket to offset estate taxes. You can usually tell who these folks are. When you look at their tax returns and inquire, you find heavy concentrations of municipal bonds and annuities. They invest in anything that will eliminate or defer income taxes.

   For such a candidate, you can often show a solution for buying insurance with some of their municipal bond interest. Or, annuitizing an annuity to pay for a life policy. Although the annuitization will create some taxes, you can show how this saves taxes in the long run and provides more total funds from a family perspective. (Annuitizing an annuity into a life policy is covered later in this this chapter.)
5. **ASSET PROTECTION.** In 2002, each person can remove $1,000,000 from an estate (plus the $11,000 annual exclusion). Those assets will no longer be subject to claims of creditors, the

guy who slips on the banana peel on their front step, or the irate garbage collector who falls and breaks his foot when your prospect's garbage can crushes it. Many prospects have a real concern about these issues, and one method of getting them moving is to segregate these assets outside of their estates. Once the funds are segregated, insurance or money management services are your follow-up recommendations.

In summarizing this list of estate planning benefits, let me briefly discuss the increase in the estate tax exemption to $3.5 million in 2009. Look at the above list and you will notice that of the five estate planning benefits for seniors, only one benefit is the saving of estate taxes. Even if estate taxes were to disappear, the reasons to do estate planning are still compelling and numerous.

If you do encounter someone who wants to procrastinate because they will sufficient relief in 2009, share these ideas:

1. "If a bus hits you tomorrow, will you owe the estate tax? Then isn't it smarter to get your affairs in order? That way, if the bus hits you, your family is set. If the exemption continues to rise and if Congress does not change the schedule, your family is still set. Heads you win, tails you win by acting now."
2. "Remember that estate taxes were liberalized under the Congress of 2001. Do you think a subsequent Congress or a new party in power can't bring them back again? Didn't Congress change the capital gains tax from 20 percent to 28 percent and back to 20 percent, and lengthen the holding period for long-term gains from twelve to eighteen and back to twelve months, all within three years? Why would you expect any change to be permanent?"
4. "Odds are estate taxes will always be with us and the pressure to increase them is constant. Why? Because only 1 to 2 percent of the U.S. population are subject to the tax, so it is an easy political target.[37] Besides, dead people don't vote!"

How to Find Estate Planning Prospects

Some financial professionals have many potential estate planning cases in their existing client records. You've sold these clients securities or insurance but have not presented or closed the estate planning business. With these people, the approach is simply to call them up: "Sheila, I was looking over your records. You have an estate planning problem. Which afternoon next week can we meet?" If Sheila is married, make sure that her spouse accompanies her to the meeting. Below, I'll explain what to do when you meet.

The other way to obtain estate planning cases is through seminars. Chapter 5 outlines the formula for successful seminars, but the most important aspect is filling up the room with qualified prospects. This is easy to do. For example, I once sent an invitation titled "Estate Planning for Residential Income Property Owners" to fifteen hundred owners of apartment buildings containing ten or more apartments. I had fifty-eight millionaires show up. Why do so many financial planners have difficulty filling up seminars? Because they do not focus their marketing. Simply look at the title I used and the group I mailed to and you can quickly see what is meant by "target marketing."

Just as with any other seminar, you must make the appointments right at the event. You cannot wait until the next day. And you must insist that anyone requesting an appointment must bring in a list of their assets and a tax return.

Your actual presentation, the content (your slides, the PowerPoint presentation, the overheads), is the least important part of the seminar, and it's the part that most planners spend the most time either creating or researching. You can obtain good presentation materials from many sources. However, without a full room of qualified attendees, the prettiest slides and the best presentation won't matter.

[37] Edward J. McCaffrey. Cato Institute Policy Analysis, No. 353.

Your First Estate Planning Meeting

Build rapport. Ask why they came to see you. Ask what's important to them about estate planning. You will need only these three tools—a current balance sheet showing net worth, a tax return, and a schedule of current estate tax rates. Review and understand the financial information, and correlate it with the prospect's answers to the questions above. At that first meeting, identify any problems and show how the family will pay unnecessary taxes. At that meeting, you can also determine the all-important emotional and psychological motivators.

- Do they want to provide for grandchildren?
- Do they have any motivation to save their children the estate tax dollars?
- What's their attitude toward income taxes?
- Do they have any charitable intent? (Ask in this way: "In your current estate plan, do you plan to leave funds to anyone or any organization other than your children?")
- Are they motivated by any of the other issues in the "What's in it for me" section?

Know that spouses may have differing views on the above issues, and you will need to sense who has more power over decisions in this arena. Additionally, if it's a second marriage, be sure you know how the asset division occurs, because the estate taxes may affect only one set of children and you will need to appeal to that parent's motives.

The first meeting gives you all the information you need for the second appointment. As the first meeting draws to a close (I highly recommend you limit it to sixty minutes), ask, "Bob and Sheila, would you like a solution to the issues we have raised today?"

If they would, you schedule a second appointment where you will provide a written recommendation. Do you need special software? As with other planning documents for seniors, I use nothing more than MS Word and MS Excel to draw up my recommendations. However, there are several estate planning software packages available.

The Second Estate Planning Meeting

Review the estate tax problem. Show them *one solution* in light of their motivators revealed in the first meeting. This is a closing meeting, and you must get some commitment for action. Those actions could include a meeting with *your* recommended estate planning attorney to draw up an irrevocable trust for gifts (or other types of trust to segregate assets), the completion of a life insurance application, or a third meeting with you if the prospects will not agree to either of the other two options.

A relationship with a local estate planning attorney you can send clients to will greatly enhance your ability to do business in the estate planning arena. That attorney will support your recommendations and act as your partner in helping you do business. How do you find such an attorney other than through a referral? Open the yellow pages and find the section titled *Attorneys, Estate Planning.* Locate those with offices near you.

WHAT TO SAY WHEN YOU CALL AN ESTATE PLANNING ATTORNEY

"Joe, my name is John Jones. I'm a financial advisor here in town with clients who need estate planning assistance. Can I buy you a sandwich next Wednesday and determine if you can help them?"

WHAT TO ASK WHEN YOU MEET

1. "Tell me about the work you do now."
2. "Do you have experience with CRTs, FLPs, QPRTs, and ILITs that allow grantors access to the assets?"
3. "Do you do business with any financial advisors?"
4. "Are you in a position to refer business for people who need financial advice?"
5. "Do you have a problem with and do you agree with the sales of insurance to pay estate taxes?"

6. "What have you seen financial planners do that you do not agree with?
7. "How do you get your clients?"
8. "Who are the two best CPAs you know in town who work with a lot of seniors?" (You will need these names for another marketing project.)

Call a new attorney each week until you find one with a personality you like and a vision of the estate planning process that matches yours. It will be easy to schedule these lunch meetings because most attorneys are interested in more business, and when you call, you make it clear that you are interested in referring clients to them.

You will also need a good insurance brokerage firm that can assist you in structuring insurance programs for estate planning cases. (If you do not already have access to such a firm, please fax for information using the fax form in the appendix.)

Investment Management

Investment management may be the ripest area in which to work with seniors. They have accumulated a large amount of investable funds, many have reached a point in life where they no longer have interest in watching the market, and others no longer have the ability to manage their own financial affairs.

As a result, many seniors are seeking the assistance of a competent investment manager to handle their portfolios.

In making any recommendation to a senior, keep a picture of a judge in your mind. Imagine yourself in a courtroom having to answer the question, "Was that a suitable recommendation?" You must always err on the side of conservatism. Portfolios for seniors should be managed with these criteria in this order:

PORTFOLIO MANAGEMENT PRIORITIES

1. No legal liability
2. Low volatility
3. High-quality securities

The goal is not to maximize returns but rather to minimize volatility and keep your client happy. Consequently, I use the low volatility Dow Dividend Strategy for many of my senior clients. Not only has the strategy beaten the S&P 500 over the last fifteen years, but our client portfolios are comprised of "sleep at night" stocks. So I recommend that the portfolios you use employ high-quality securities that will produce happy clients for many years.

Long-Term Care

Long-term care holds the greatest promise in the insurance industry. The population of senior buyers is growing rapidly, and the product is now at its explosion phase. Currently only 10 percent of people over age sixty-four have obtained such insurance.[38] Like other products that get to a 10 percent penetration level, they quickly blast off as the word of mouth of critical mass produces soaring product volume.

Incredible as it may seem, there are still seniors who believe that Medicare will pay for long-term care needs. Others realize that the government will not pay, but have procrastinated taking on another insurance obligation of $100 to $200 per month. But it's only a matter of time until most seniors have a spouse, friend, or relative requiring long-term care and they all rush to get protection. Soon, doing without long-term care insurance will be considered as foolish as going without medical insurance.

How is this market best pursued? Let's look at an approach that failed and an approach that succeeds.

[38] Bests Review, October 1999.

A short time ago, I visited an office of a well-known major insurance company. They had decided to make a big cut into the long-term care market. They opened eight offices across the country specializing in long-term care. Their marketing system was to send a lot of mail (poorly written direct mail that stressed the facts and forgot the emotions) and have telemarketers call the reply cards that came back and schedule appointments for the licensed agents. Then the agents would go out on the appointments to the senior's home. When a sale was made, the compensation structure to the agent was horrendous—the agent received 30 percent of the premium as commission. Since most of the agents had been recruited from the life insurance side of the business (where they were accustomed to commission rates of 60 to 90 percent), the commission rates at this division were considered abysmal. Additionally, independent agents on the outside were getting commission rates of 50 to 75 percent.

The firm was committed to this one method of mailing, telemarketing, and having the agents meet with prospects in their homes. This method is similar to that used by many roofing and siding companies, yet was being employed to sell a complex product that was new and had high perceived risk (i.e., the risk of a bad choice could leave the insured without coverage when they really needed it).

Although this firm is one of the top five life insurance companies in the United States, their name never appears on a list of even the top twenty long-term care insurers, and they are a non-existent player in the market. To my knowledge, these long-term care offices have been closed.

STRATEGIC ERRORS IN OFFERING LONG-TERM CARE INSURANCE

- The direct mail was poorly constructed and response rates were low.
- Telemarketers cannot be used to set appointments for complex products. Many sales professionals will admit they are very good

once they get in front of a prospect; it's getting the appointment that's difficult. This being the case, isn't it a mistake to put a non-salesperson on the phone to make the appointments?

- By providing inferior compensation, the quality of professional was low and the firm was unable to attract top-quality talent.

Now let's see how another large insurer played the same game.

They also mail to hundreds of thousands of seniors (ages sixty to seventy-five). The firm has a highly recognizable and well-respected name. The mailing piece offers a quotation for insurance. The reply cards received are given directly to the agents to make their own appointments.

The agents at this firm are also compensated poorly—25 percent first-year commission (as compared to 50 to 75 percent that independent agents receive). As a result, turnover is very high. However, from the insurer's standpoint, the turnover of agents may not be a problem as, once the policies are sold, a low percentage are cancelled. Of course, the most successful agents go independent for the higher compensation.

This successful company essentially did one important thing differently: It had the agents set their own appointments. By realizing that "selling" an appointment to a senior requires professional sales talent, they have prospered where the other, equally financially endowed competitor failed.

Let me tell you about an agent who has sold four hundred long-term care policies *annually* for the last several years. She does something that's very simple, yet many agents just never do it. She replicates the same system used by the large successful insurance company, but does it a little better.

She purchases a list of senior homeowners, aged sixty-five to seventy-four, having household incomes of $35,000+. By qualifying her prospects by income, she is more certain that they can afford insurance. (The insurance companies mentioned above used no income qualification.) She also uses a narrower age range: slightly older to increase seeing motivated prospects. To prospect a younger audience for long-term care is foolish. It's not that younger people don't need to have this coverage, and it makes most sense for them to buy it at an early age. But remember our earlier marketing principle of selling food where people are hungry? You want to present long-term care protection to people who have aches and pains, and have friends and relatives that are starting to have significant health problems. Until they identify with the problem personally and emotionally, there's no motivation, and there's no sale! Therefore, if you want to serve people by selling long-term care, your most motivated prospects will be in the sixty-five to seventy-four age group.

Every eight weeks, the successful advisor mails seventy-five hundred two-part direct response cards that require recipients to fill in their birth dates and phone numbers to receive a comparative analysis of policies. Many agents would never think of spending $3,000 to $4,000 every eight weeks. That's why many agents aren't making the kind of money this woman does: $400,000 to 500,000 annually.

She gets a 4 percent response to her mailing—people who complete their birth date and phone number and request a quote. She then proceeds to follow up on those leads within twenty-four hours of receipt to schedule an appointment in their home. If she is asked to mail something, she explains that would be a disservice. If they want to have more answers and fewer questions, she needs to meet with them.

This top professional schedules her appointments three days of each week and does the business of eight average agents. She understands the simple and critical truth that unless the risk is personalized by the prospect, there's no sale. She is a master at asking three important questions to personalize the risk.

HER SECRET: EMOTION, NOT REASON

Ask your prospects these emotional questions:

- "Do you want to be a burden on your family?"
- "If you went into a nursing home, how long would your money last before you needed to sell your home?"
- "What experience have you or someone you know had with long-term care?"

Personally, I find long-term care insurance to be one of the easiest sales for these reasons.

LONG-TERM CARE CAN BE AN EASY SALE

1. **POSITION IT AS AN EXTENSION TO HEALTH INSURANCE.** You can ask them if they realize their health insurance is deficient and does not cover the *effects* of many illnesses. For example, if they were to have a stroke, their insurance would cover a few days in the hospital. But when they go home and they have no use of their right leg, how will they shop, cook, and clean? Their health insurance policy will not cover the full impact of the illness. The same is true of Parkinson's, chronic arthritis, osteoporosis, and any other debilitating condition of the skeletal, muscular, or nervous system.
2. **SENIORS AVOID MAKING IRREVERSIBLE FINANCIAL DECISIONS.** The purchase of long-term care insurance is *reversible* because it takes four weeks for the insurer to process the application, and the prospect has a thirty-day "free-look" window in which to make a permanent decision. With this flexibility, it's easy for me to have prospects move forward with an application, as they know they have the right to reverse their decision over the next sixty days.

In discussing financial protection for long-term care needs, some people ask me why they shouldn't wait to buy a long-term care policy.

"After all," they argue, "Each year I wait, I can invest the money that would have been spent on insurance." At first, this argument may make sense, but it loses its validity when I ask this person if they do the same with their homeowners insurance.

The problem with any insurable risk is that you never know when the problem will strike. In the case of long-term care, the "problem" may not be a long-term care need. It could merely be some condition that appears in your medical records that makes you uninsurable—forever. Therefore, the real risk of waiting is becoming uninsurable. Fact: In California, insurers reject one in four applicants, according to the findings of the California Partnership for Long-Term Care. In many cases, applicants are rejected simply because they have waited too long and their health records contain negative information.

As with any insurance, you have to get it when you don't need it because insurance companies do not sell insurance to people who need it (e.g., try and buy homeowners insurance while your house is burning down).

The chances of becoming uninsurable aside, doesn't it make financial sense to wait? Here are figures for a fifty-five-year-old man who decided to wait until he was seventy. For fifteen years, he invested the money at 5 percent.

	AGE 55	**AGE 70**
Annual Premium[39]	$ 470	$ 2,026
Total Payments to Age 80	11,750	20,260
Money Invested and Accumulated		-9,411
Net Cost	11,750	10,849

As the above table shows, the savings for waiting 15 years is $1,100. Is the 50% chance of having a long-term care incident after age 65 and being uninsured worth $1,100?

Tell your clients, "We would be delighted to review your long-term care options now and help you avoid the higher risk of waiting."

[39] Bankers United Personal Choice (GC-RB-PC-Mpref-CA-501) rates as of 1/28/02, zero elimination days, 5% simple inflation option, $100/day benefit, 1500 day term, 100% home care option.

Immediate Annuities

Immediate annuities have become unpopular over the past several years. Many people do not like the fact that if they died an early death, the insurance company would keep their money. However, innovations in this product, which I have not seen widely advertised, make it much more attractive. A handful of insurance companies will guarantee that the original deposit is always returned—the "refund provision." It works as follows.

At age seventy, Mrs. Jones deposits $100,000, in return for a monthly income of $1,000 for as long as she lives. After four years, she passes away. With the refund provision, her heirs will continue to receive $1,000 per month for another fifty-two months ($100,000 less the $48,000 received by Mrs. Jones) until the entire investment has been recovered.

The other objection to immediate annuities has been that payments are fixed, and fixed income may not be beneficial during periods of inflation. Here again the insurance industry has responded to this issue. It offers immediate variable annuities with the monthly payments tied to the performance of the investment subaccounts selected by the investor. If the subaccounts rise, payments rise. The opposite is also true (with a guaranteed minimum fixed payment provided, regardless of subaccount performance).

Health-adjusted SPIAs: Poor Health Can Be a Factor in Producing More Income

There's a type of annuity that pays more if the annuitant's health profile is not good. It's an immediate annuity with health underwriting.

Take this hypothetical example. A seventy-year-old man decides to obtain a single premium investment annuity (SPIA). He deposits a $100,000 premium and, based on his standard life expectancy of sixteen years, his monthly payment is $761.20 (a 9.1% percent annual payout rate). He will receive this fixed monthly amount regardless of how long he lives.

However, if he has a negative health profile and the insurance companies calculate his life expectancy at only ten years, his monthly payment will jump to $975.80. Because of the negative health history, this annuitant receives more income.

Additionally, if your prospect has been relying on municipal bonds for tax-sheltered income, the same funds in a health-adjusted SPIA can often bring more income.

Let's take a look again at the hypothetical case of Mr. Jones, age seventy, with a $500,000 portfolio of municipal bonds, earning 5 percent tax-free. He receives $25,000 of annual tax-free income.

If his health qualifies him for a health-adjusted SPIA, he could get $58,548 annually for the same $500,000. (The exact amount depends on an analysis of his medical records by the annuity company.) Of this amount, approximately 68 percent is not taxable, so his net after-tax income would be $52,182. His spendable income increases by $27,182 annually, without the risk of changing interest rates, bond defaults in his portfolio, or the trouble of handling maturing issues.

However, remember that an immediate annuity does not leave anything for the heirs. So Mr. Jones does the following with his additional $27,182 annually: he keeps $7,182 for himself and takes an extra cruise, and he gifts the other $20,000 annually to his children. They, in turn, purchase a life insurance policy on Mrs. Jones, who is in good health. In these circumstances, the policy would provide a death benefit exceeding $890,000[40] guaranteed to age one-hundred.

In this scenario, Mr. Jones has captured more income for his own needs and provided an additional $390,000 tax-free death benefit to his children.

Certificates of Deposit

No financial advisor will get rich providing certificates of deposit, but they are an excellent way to start a relationship with a senior.

[40] Lincoln Benefit Life, 02/05/02, SPIA rated to age 80

I spent four years providing investments and investment advice in a bank environment, so I became aware of the investing habits of many seniors firsthand. Several were "CD shoppers." They went from bank to bank or called around town to find where they could get the highest-paying CDs. Although many securities firms offer CDs from several banks, I never see this service advertised. (I have seen securities firms advertise a particular CD, but never the service of proving rates from fifty institutions, custodianship of all CDs in one account, one 1099 form, easy ability to roll over by phone with the bank paying the best rate, and all interest funneled into one account.) Advertising this CD shopping service is an excellent way to meet seniors and start a relationship.

The fixed income desk at your broker-dealer should have information about these CDs, or if you're independent, contact LaSalle Bank at (800) 327-1546.

Financial Techniques for the Senior Market

While the previous section discussed products and services, this section will focus on approaches that are of unique benefit to seniors. Many of these deal with generating more income. Although few affluent seniors need more income, they usually like it.

Capital Gains Elimination Trust

This trust is a charitable remainder trust (CRT). I promise that if you start off presenting any approach with the word *charitable,* you will lose your prospects' attention. For many people, charitable means "giving my money away." Before they hear the benefits, they will stop listening. Most prospects and planners do not realize that actuarial structure requires that only 10 percent of the principal donated to such a trust must pass to the charity. So for the first fifteen minutes of your presentation, I encourage you to call this a *capital gains elimination trust.* You will have more attentive prospects.

A VERY POWERFUL TOOL FOR SENIORS WHO . . .

- Want to turn raw land into an income stream and avoid the capital gains tax
- Want to liquidate hassle assets (e.g., residential rental property) and boost their income stream while avoiding the capital gains tax
- Want to convert non-dividend or low-dividend stock into income assets and avoid the capital gains tax
- Want an estate planning tool that will remove assets from their estate without removing the income

You can obtain further details from Renaissance at (317) 843-5400.

Charitable gift annuities work in a similar fashion, and most charities will structure these to offer the above benefits. The charitable gift annuity is simpler (there is no trust required) but also has less flexibility for your client.

Using a Single Premium Immediate Annuity to Fund Long-term Care

Many seniors are reluctant to take on additional monthly payments. Thus, there is some resistance to obtaining long-term care (LTC) coverage. Some smart LTC insurers have started offering the single payment option with no need for continuing payments.

You can also structure this for your clients. Rather than having them make annual payments, just make a single deposit into an immediate annuity. The annual annuity payments will pay for the LTC insurance. (Note that the payments on the LTC insurance can rise, but the payments from the immediate annuity are fixed.)

A woman I met in her early seventies expressed interest to me in long-term care coverage that would cost about $1,000 annually. She said she already felt poor and did not want to spend any money on insurance. I noticed, however, that among her many assets was a small $10,000 annuity, so I asked her if she ever withdrew any money from it. She said no, and I pointed out the following idea:

Annuitize the annuity for life. Such an annuity would generate a lifetime payout of approximately $1,000 annually—just the amount needed to get important long-term care coverage. This is money she is not using anyway, so it has no effect on her spending. By committing this small asset, this $10,000 annuity, it will fund her long-term care premiums for life (assuming level premiums).

You can explain to your clients that there will be some taxes on an immediate annuity income that are affected by age and basis in the contract. The bottom line, however, is that this technique works very well to get people the protection they need without the burden of annual recurring payments.

Convert Annuities to Life Insurance

I often meet seniors who own annuities. They purchased the annuity as a means to keep funds safe and have the fund grow tax-deferred. I ask when they plan on using these funds. Sometimes they tell me they have no reason to use the annuity, and it will pass along in their estate. I ask them if they would like to pass along possibly three times as much.

I then show them how to annuitize (typically over five to seven years to make a non-modified endowment contract life policy) the annuity into a life insurance policy. If the policy is owned outside of their estate, it pays off income tax-free and passes estate tax-free to their heirs. It is true that my clients will need to pay any deferred tax each time a payment transfers from the annuity to the life policy. However, I always have the annuity company withhold this at the source so my client will not have any out-of-pocket taxes. I structure the life insurance premiums to equal the after-tax annuity distributions.

In many cases, the benefit to the heirs is three to four times the after-tax amount that would have been inherited from the annuity.

Reducing Taxes on IRA Distributions

Many financial planners are touting the "stretch IRA," and this is a good idea. The stretch IRA is simply the idea of establishing an IRA so that whatever you do not use can compound tax deferred for a very long period (maybe two additional generations). This is done by proper naming of the beneficiaries and insuring that beneficiaries make use of disclaimers when appropriate. Success also requires that heirs be educated not to liquidate the IRA all at once and pay a chunk of tax, but rather, enjoy the lifetime deferral that the IRS allows.

An even more powerful solution are the strategies in the Advanced IRA Distribution Strategy offered by NF Communications. To get information on this package, please fax the form in the appendix.

With one of these strategies, the prospect purchases a life insurance policy in his retirement plan. Because of the way life insurance is taxed when distributed from a retirement plan, he pays tax on only a fraction of each dollar invested. Then, he gifts the policy to his heirs using the one-time estate exclusion or annual exclusions.

Result? The prospect has saved a lot of taxes for himself and has saved estate taxes for the children by removing the policy from the estate. What if he wants to use some of the cash? No problem. He leaves some of the money in the plan for spending and uses these strategies for the part of the plan he has no plans to consume.

Chapter 7 Summary

There are a number of under-utilized and poorly sold financial products, such as reverse mortgages, that you can reposition and maximize for use by seniors. In addition, services traditionally sought by seniors, such as estate planning, can be offered in such a way as to increase their value to seniors. Use the strategies in this chapter to offer financial solutions mature clients want and need.

8 Position Yourself As an Expert

One method of making all of your advertising and marketing efforts pay off is to be seen by your prospects as an expert.

It's been said that seniors are the last generation of readers, and they believe and trust what they read. Therefore, if you want to position yourself as an expert in the senior market, become the author of books, newsletters, booklets, pamphlets—anything that appears to be professionally published. That doesn't mean you have to do the writing. There is a large cottage industry in America of ghostwriters.

In fact, there are plenty of quality newsletters, booklets, and entire books that have already been professionally written but can be customized with your picture and biography, making you the overnight author. (Usually, you would need to disclose, in a footnote or something similar, that they have been written by others.) To ethically claim expert knowledge, you should have mastery over the published material. The appendix provides more information on where to get books already ghostwritten for you.

Being an expert also includes having items written about you. When you are quoted in articles or other news items, you are assumed to be the expert. Getting interviewed by local reporters is easy once you know how. Journalists are always looking for news and depend on professionals like you to supply it. They need you, and you can start being the source of news for them.

The secondary benefit of these kinds of publicity is that you can use published items in your sales and marketing materials. Every time you send a letter to someone or have a seminar, give out copies of articles written about or by you. Nothing builds your credibility faster.

The News Release

The primary tool for getting the press to pay attention to you is the news release. By sending a news release every month, you'll show reporters and editors that you are a local professional they can rely upon. The secrets of getting interviewed are consistency, newsworthiness, the proper format, and sending it to the right person. Let's look at all four elements.

Finding the Right Contacts

You will need to call each of the newspapers, radio stations, and television stations in your local market. Consult your phone book or go to the library, where you will find a local directory of all of the media outlets in your area. Look in a copy of the *Gale Directory* of publications and broadcast media or *Ulrich's International Periodicals Directory.*

Call to ask for the name of the reporter or editor who should receive news releases on senior issues. Also ask for the person who should receive information on personal financial issues. These may be two different people working on two different sections of the paper. For example, financial planning issues may be handled in the business section, while senior issues may be handled by the lifestyles or human interest editor. It's okay if you have two different contacts at the same organization. They will both get your materials each month. Be sure to enter all contact information into your database: name, address, phone, fax, e-mail address, etc.

Each month, send a news release (see exhibit 1 for proper format) focusing on an issue affecting seniors. At first, you may think there is no way you can find a new issue each month affecting seniors. However, there are many topics that may not seem like senior issues but do affect the senior crowd.

IN THE NEWS: AFFECTING SENIORS

As I write this in late 1999 and early 2000, these are recent issues affecting seniors that have been in the news:

- Congress' proposal to eliminate the estate tax
- Elimination of the earnings ceiling for seniors' collection of social security benefits
- The Treasury's delay in issuing regulations regarding the taxability of non-qualified long-term care policies
- The National Association of Securities Dealers' warning to member firms about inappropriate sales of variable annuities into IRAs or qualified plans
- The extension of time (until December 31, 1999) to re-convert a Roth IRA

Although these may not at first appear to be senior issues, they do impact seniors to a large extent and are fertile topics for news releases. Our firm issued news releases on all of these issues in 1999 (a service you can subscribe to for getting yourself local publicity—from NF Communications as described in the appendix).

The time-sensitive nature of the news release demands immediate attention and requests the reporter to call you. Here's a perfect example: In the summer of 1998, the stock market started caving in. I sent a news release about how seniors' portfolios had become too bloated with equities and seniors were particularly vulnerable (because they need to protect capital). Smack in the middle of a bear market, the article appeared: "Ride Out Market Fluctuations, Financial Planner Says." The article was an interview with me alone; no other professional was mentioned. I gave the reporter exactly what she was seeking at the right time. That's the power of a good news release.

Just start sending a monthly news release. Once you are recognized as a knowledgeable professional, within three to four months you will start getting calls from the press about interviews or asking to use one of your articles.

Why does it take so long to get results?

Understand what happens when you send your materials. Reporters will receive your information and file it in a subject file. For example, they may have been thinking about a story on long-term care, so they start a file and dump stuff into it. Along comes your item on long-term care, and they dump that into the file. Four months later, they realize they have a big file on long-term care and enough material to do a story. They flip through it looking for people to interview, and there's your news release or article.

The Format of a News Release

Accompany your news release with your biography (exhibit B) and a list of questions for the reporter to ask you (exhibit C). By giving reporters a list of questions, you make it easy for them to interview you.

I am often asked if credentials will influence a reporter to call. The answer is that they can, but credentials are not a significant factor in how much publicity you can generate or how successful you can be. Your expertise is a function of perception, and by writing a strong biography (as illustrated in exhibit E), you can generate a very solid impression regardless of your credentials.

Do not expect that sending news releases will work all the time or that results are immediate. This takes a little time, but with consistency, you will get calls. Your assistant can perform the mechanical process of mailing or faxing the news release each month. You do not need to spend your time.

In a very short while, you will be a well-known financial expert in your community. Most important, when you distribute your articles at seminars or send them to prospects, you will open more new accounts faster and more easily.

Use Professional Communications Models

One pages 126–137 are sample documents for your reference in creating your own materials. Or, if you prefer, you can contact us at NF Communications, Inc., to assist you.

- **EXHIBIT A, NEWS RELEASES.** Send a news release, along with documents like exhibits B and C, to the people on your press list. Or if you subscribe with NF Communications, Inc., you can receive a copy of a news release each month. (See information on the Public Relations Kit in the appendix.)
- **EXHIBIT B, BIOGRAPHY.** Develop a strong biography. Exhibit E includes additional sample biographies. Please use them as templates for your own.
- **EXHIBIT C, SUGGESTED QUESTIONS.** This list of questions makes it easy for a reporter to interview you. We can supply this to you each month.
- **EXHIBIT D, ANSWERS TO SUGGESTED QUESTIONS.** Reporters do not see this list. It is a copy of the questions you sent with your answers already typed out. That way, when they call you on the phone and start asking you these questions, you pull out the answers and sound like the super professional that you are.
- **EXHIBIT E, SAMPLE BIOGRAPHIES.**

EXHIBIT A

NEWS RELEASE #1

FOR IMMEDIATE RELEASE

FOR FURTHER INFORMATION
CALL LARRY KLEIN (555) 999-9999

Seniors Unaware of Risks to Their Assets

Many retired investors have found refuge in mutual funds in the last few years and have been well rewarded. The looming problem is a market decline that could financially and emotionally devastate this group. Many senior investors have no idea that their funds could lose 40 to 50 percent of their value in a short period even those funds billed as conservative funds. They have been ill-informed of the risk and history of their investments, says Larry Klein, CPA, MBA, Registered Investment Advisor. Just look at the record of the last bear market and how leading funds reacted.

	1973	1974
Vanguard Windsor	-25.02	-16.80
Vanguard Wellington	-11.83	-17.73
Alliance Quasar	-23.16	-43.38
American Mutual	-10.70	-15.93
Davis NY Venture	-23.98	-20.17
Fundamental Investors	-27.03	-26.36
Mairs & Power Growth	-25.12	-34.25
Nicholas	-52.70	-33.44
Sife Trust	-18.00	-34.96

Source: *Morningstar Principia*, Advanced Analytics

Larry Klein recently published *Retirement Investing* and is the author of several articles on estate planning. He is also a well-known Bay Area educator, whose classes include Retirement Investing and Investing in Securities at UC Berkeley. He has helped thousands of seniors navigate their financial affairs. He is a CPA and Harvard MBA.

For an interview, phone him at (555) 999-9999.

# # #

For news releases sent to a radio station, also include the following.

Suggested Introduction for Larry Klein

Mr. Klein is a CPA, Harvard MBA, Certified Senior Advisor and Registered Investment Advisor. In 1988, he was named Outstanding Broker by *Registered Representative* magazine, the leading trade journal for the stock brokerage industry. That designation is awarded to only ten people in the nation each year.

He is an expert in financial matters as they affect seniors, the fastest growing segment of the population. His firm, Senior Resources, is located in Walnut Creek.

Be sure to have a pen and paper handy. He ll be giving you information you won t want to miss.

NEWS RELEASE #2

FOR IMMEDIATE RELEASE

FOR FURTHER INFORMATION
CALL LARRY KLEIN (555) 999-9999

Your Grandmother Could Go to Jail

In its infinite wisdom, Congress has passed a law that could have grandmothers going to jail. It is now a felony to make a gift to one s family for the purpose of reducing one s assets and then later applying for Medicaid. This is an absolutely ludicrous law, says Larry Klein, CPA, MBA, and Registered Investment Advisor. Congress is frustrated by the amount of money being spent by Medicaid. Rather than rewrite the rules, they have instituted some pecuniary punishment for those foolish enough to be caught by them. The Medicaid rules are so bad, I could show anyone, with any size estate, how to legally qualify for Medicaid. Unfortunately, some poor souls unaware of this law could get thrown in jail.

Larry Klein recently published *Retirement Investing* and is the author of several articles on estate planning. He is also a well-known Bay Area educator, whose classes include Retirement Investing and Investing in Securities at UC Berkeley. He has helped thousands of seniors navigate their financial affairs. He is a CPA and Harvard MBA.

For an interview, phone him at (555) 999-9999.

# # #

EXHIBIT B

BIOGRAPHY

LARRY KLEIN, CPA, MBA

BIOGRAPHY AND FACT SHEET

Larry Klein is recognized as a leading financial educator in the Bay Area. In addition to his book, *Retirement Investing*, he has published several articles on estate planning and has been written about in many local and national publications, including *Registered Representative* and *Viewpoint*, the CNA agent magazine. He has also taught a class called Retirement Investing at several adult schools and the Investing in Securities course at the University of California at Berkeley.

Mr. Klein is a CPA, Harvard MBA, Certified Senior Advisor, and Registered Investment Advisor. In 1988, he was named Outstanding Broker by *Registered Representative* magazine, the leading trade journal for the stock brokerage industry. That designation is awarded to only ten people in the nation each year.

He is an expert in financial matters as they affect seniors, the fastest growing segment of the population.

He founded NF Communications, (*www.nfcom.com*), which provides marketing tools that help stockbrokers, financial planners, investment advisors, and insurance agents to increase their client base and their income.

Larry Klein

(555) 999-9999

EXHIBIT C

SUGGESTED QUESTIONS

Suggested Questions for Larry Klein
Author of *Retirement Investing*

I understand there will be some grandmothers thrown in jail after January 1. What s this all about?

Why does this law exist?

What can seniors do about it?

Does this impact all seniors equally?

What are the other options for long-term health care other than Medicaid?

Are there other areas that have negative implications of which most seniors are unaware?

What estate planning ideas do most seniors miss?

How can people get your book?

I understand that seniors are particularly vulnerable to any stock market downturn.
Why is that?

Is it true that many retirees do not understand their investments? Is there evidence of that?

Has the mutual fund industry hidden or obscured the risk in mutual fund investing?

What should retirees be doing to protect their investments?

Are there any rules they can follow?

Are there particular investments better designed or more suitable for retirees?

What has changed about this issue in the last ten years?

EXHIBIT D

ANSWERS TO SUGGESTED QUESTIONS

Suggested questions for Larry Klein
Author of *Retirement Investing*

I understand there will be some grandmothers thrown in jail after January 1. What s this all about?

Starting January 1, if a senior gives a gift and then needs to apply for Medicaid assistance in the following three years, that gift will be considered a felony, a criminal act punishable by imprisonment.

Why does this law exist?

As you know, most government programs that fill senior needs are going broke. Medicaid is no exception. In the past, some people have abused the Medicaid system by giving their money away, then they were able to qualify to get Medicaid payments to pay for nursing home costs, for example. The government wanted to stop such abuse so they made such gifts within three years of applying for Medicaid a criminal act.

What can seniors do about it?

The simple answer is to not make any gifts. For those who do make gifts, keep very good records and documentation of the reason. Be able to show that the intent was not to qualify for Medicaid, that the gift was for a birthday or Christmas, that the gift was small in relation to your net worth, or that the gift was for other estate planning purposes.

Does this impact all seniors equally?

No. It impacts people who are likely to need Medicaid support the poor. People who are never going to apply for Medicaid because they have enough of their own resources to pay for a nursing home, which runs about $4,000 a month in the Bay Area, or someone who has purchased long-term care insurance, will most likely never use the Medicaid system. They are unaffected by this law.

What are the other options for long-term health care other than Medicaid?

For the poor, Medicaid is the backstop. It s there to take care of people when they run out of money. I advise middle-income people to obtain long-term care insurance. It s less expensive than most people think and it covers seniors for a very substantial risk. For those with higher incomes or net worths, they might be able to afford the $4,000 a month from their own resources, which I call self-insurance.

Are there other areas that have negative implications of which most seniors are unaware?

Yes, I find that seniors make errors in several areas of estate planning. Here s a common one. Seniors will place the names of children on bank accounts. They do this so that, should the senior pass away, the child inherits the bank account without probate. This is correct. But let s say the child has a legal problem and gets sued. The assets get attached, and that bank account could also get attached because the child s name is on the account. This act places a senior s assets in danger unnecessarily. If people want to avoid probate, which is almost always a good idea, that s what living trusts are for.

What estate planning ideas do most seniors miss?

Here in the Bay Area, there are lots of seniors with assets in excess of $600,000. Each dollar over $600,000 is subject to estate taxes. I find that many families end up paying estate taxes when they could have easily been avoided by some simple estate planning, such as using living trusts, or gifting, or using insurance to pay the taxes. These are all simple ideas, yet because people often do not want to face the discussion of their own mortality, these ideas go unexplored and the family loses financially.

How can people get your book?

That s easy. Simply call (800) xxx-xxxx. Just leave your address and credit card number. The book is $16 with taxes and shipping included. Or people can send a check to Larry Klein at:

1700 North Broadway, Suite 405
Walnut Creek, CA 94596

You would continue with this document, answering all questions you proposed in exhibit C.

EXHIBIT E

SAMPLE BIOGRAPHIES

It does not matter how much experience you have; you can make yourself sound like someone worth talking to. Follow some basic rules:

1. Do not start with your title and broker dealer.
2. Leave your accomplishments and everything about you to the second half of the biography. Use the first half to tell readers what you can do for them.
3. Always close your biography with an item of personal interest (e.g., where you live, about your spouse, your kids, etc.).

Your biography should give the reader background information on your credentials, education, how you assist your clients, lectures/classes you've taught, articles/books you have written, etc. Use some of this language or alter it to your benefit. You do not need lots of credentials or experience. If you use the following samples as a guideline, you will sound like a professional worth consulting.

BAD BIOGRAPHY

Joe Smith is a stockbroker with Merrill Lynch. He holds an insurance license and series 7 and series 63 licenses. Joe is also a Certified Financial Planner. Joe has given seminars at major employers in the area. He has been a broker for the last five years and is a graduate of Winnetka University.

What's wrong with this biography? It talks about the stuff Joe wants to sell you (stocks and insurance). It covers something the prospect has no interest in, and many readers will not even know what a Certified Financial Planner is. This biography lends no credibility to Joe and takes away credibility by telling you he has only five years in the business and attended an unknown university. Does the prospect know what the series 7 and 63 are? I don't think so.

GOOD BIOGRAPHY

Joe Smith, a well-known financial educator in Torrance, teaches retirement classes that have been widely attended by retirees from Lockheed, TRW and Disney. He has developed a specialty in working with retirees, and those about to retire, who want to protect their principal and ensure that their money lasts. Joe helps investors avoid the common mistakes made by most retirees, and he explains how he has counseled hundreds to avoid these pitfalls. If you attend one workshop this year looking for ways to help protect your capital, don't miss Joe Smith's presentation.

Joe has helped people cut their taxes by as much as 50 percent, avoid taxes on social security income, avoid estate taxes, and protect their estate values. Investors that have used his advice include retired government employees, retired teachers, physicians, and business executives approaching retirement.

Joe is a graduate of Louisiana State University, where he majored in finance and earned his MBA. He has used his financial acumen to benefit the community as treasurer of the Mobile League and member of the Baton Rouge Rotary. Joe is also a Certified Financial Planner, which required him to take an eighteen-month course of study and pass six rigorous exams, proving his comprehensive knowledge of personal financial issues.

Joe lives with his wife, Molly, who is a geriatric nurse at Torrance Hospital, and his two daughters in the Rivers area. Joe's hobby, when he's not making people richer, is reducing his handicap at Brown Oaks Golf Course.

Please note that only one paragraph of this biography mentions credentials, colleges, and certifications. If these were omitted, the biography would still make Joe sound like a guy you want to hear. You don't need fancy degrees or credentials with a good biography. Please note that if you have given at least one seminar before, and employees of some large companies have attended, the second sentence in the above biography is true. (Omit the word "widely" if that is an overstatement.)

If you participate in relevant community activities that make you sound like a good citizen (the soccer team coach, member of Rotary, etc.), add them.

Use pieces of the preceding biography to create one good paragraph for your news releases.

More Sample Biographies

Larry Jones has been assisting seniors for twelve years to protect their assets and reduce risk. In fact, over one thousand retirees have used Larry's advice to safely invest over $500 million into secure investments, such as annuities and fixed income investments. Retirees of IBM, AT&T, Chevron, and General Electric have sought his advice. Larry is regarded as an expert in capital preservation for retirees.

Larry is a well-known financial educator and writes regular columns, in print and on the Internet, about conservative investments. Larry regularly holds presentations on various topics which are widely attended by people aged fifty-five to eighty who are looking ahead for their own welfare. Readers are invited to call for a free copy of Larry's booklet, Avoiding Mistakes with Long-Term Care Insurance. *You can call toll free at (888) 888-8888 and ask to receive a free newsletter, or find out about scheduling Larry as a speaker for your group or organization.*

Neal Nickity has been assisting senior investors for the last fifteen years. Mr. Nickity started his career as an accountant with a large aerospace firm and moved into advising individuals as a vice president of investments at Great Western Financial Securities and then

American Savings Bank Financial Services. In 1990, the leading magazine for the bank brokerage industry selected Neal as one of the Ten Outstanding Investment Brokers in the United States based on client service. Mr. Nickity is a Certified Financial Planner (which required completion of two years of study and passing six exams).

Neal has lectured widely on financial topics at Mission College and College of the Canyons. His "Retirement Investing" class has been widely attended in the Los Angeles area.

Neal is the author of Retirement Investing, *an easy-to-read book suited for those already retired or close to retirement. His articles on estate planning and retirement investing have been published in local newspapers. His free newsletter is available by contacting the author at (888) 888-8888.*

Bill Butler is a well-known financial educator in Olympia, Washington. His retirement seminars have been widely attended by retirees from the Boeing Company, Microsoft Corporation, and Weyerhaeuser Company. Bill has developed a specialty in working with retirees and those about to retire who want to protect their principal and ensure that their money lasts. His expertise is advising seniors to avoid the common mistakes made by most retirees.

Bill has helped people cut their taxes by as much as 50 percent, avoid taxes on social security, avoid estate taxes, and protect their estates. Bill and his wife, Phyllis, have one child and live in the South Sound area.

Marvin Constance is a well-known local expert in the matters of senior investors. Since 1988, he has taught retirement planning classes on the Monterey Peninsula. He assists investors aged sixty-plus to preserve their capital, increase their income, and more profitably structure their investments. People who consult Marvin find that they lower their tax bills by as much as 50 percent, eliminate taxes on their social security income, increase their fixed monthly income, and obtain better protection for their financial future.

Mr. Constance has been providing consulting services to seniors for thirty years. He has been a nursing home administrator and is one of only 8000 Certified Senior Advisors in the nation. To become a Certified Senior Advisor, he completed a fifteen-part program of study in the financial, physical, emotional, and personal issues of seniors.

Another Must for Promoting Yourself: Send a Newsletter

How many times has the following happened to you?

You meet prospects but they do not make an appointment. Or, you have appointments but they decide not to take action. So you put their contact information into your tickler for a call in ninety days. When you call them in three months, you find out one has just invested $100,000 into an annuity that would have grossed you $8,000. But she had forgotten about you. In fact, she says, "Gee, Joe, I would have made this investment with you, but the guy at the bank caught me when I was rolling over a CD."

If you want to maximize the yield from your seminars, direct mail, or any other marketing program, it's critical to keep in contact with people you have met but who did not make an appointment or become a client. Eventually they will. You have to be in front of them *at the right time and with the right message.*

If you fail to maintain contact, the above scenario will happen to you again and again. Money, transactions, policies, and commissions will continue to slip through your fingers.

This is where most financial professionals fall down. They waste significant prospecting effort meeting people yet never bring them to full boil. They waste time and energy heating the water yet fail to keep the flame burning. Their hot prospects simply evaporate. Read on and see how the right newsletter can convert these prospects to clients.

A monthly direct response newsletter will help you turn prospects into clients. Why monthly? Because people have a lot of distractions in life, and they see lots of offers and advertisements. After thirty days, they barely remember who you are. But by having your newsletter show up in their mailbox once a month, you stay fresh on their minds.

If you do not keep in touch with clients and prospects, know that someone else will. Another financial professional will invite your clients to seminars and keep after them with their newsletter, and your clients' assets and prospect base will drift elsewhere. The only efficient way to stay in front of your prospects and clients is with a monthly newsletter.

Sending just any newsletter will not do the job. If you want to focus on the senior market, then the newsletter must be devoted to senior issues.

APPROPRIATE TOPICS FOR A SENIOR NEWSLETTER

- Tax reduction
- Long-term care
- Health issues
- Estate planning
- Growth investing
- Income investing
- Asset protection

You've seen the kind of newsletters most professionals send: some boring junk about a change in the tax law, the latest economic report, statistics from the fed, political commentary. Such a newsletter will not inspire people to contact you.

Prospects think only one thing, *What's in it for me?* They couldn't care less about some economic prognostication or the change in the fed funds rate. They want to know, "How am I gonna make more money?" Or in the case of seniors, they ask, "How can I best preserve my principal and obtain more income?"

So I recommend you send a newsletter that tells them point-blank how they can make money or save it. Every article should answer the question, "What's in it for me?" As a result, the newsletter generates business for you. People respond (by the reply coupon) and they call. A good newsletter is a silent salesperson for you.

If you just send a newsletter with some interesting information but do not call the reader to action (e.g., send back the coupon for more information), your newsletter will be a waste of your money. You must get the reader to *respond!*

Many professionals have no idea how to use their newsletter to make them money. These professionals think that somehow they will profit by sending a nice, four-page newsletter with their picture, a newsletter that contains articles unrelated to their clients' and prospects' concerns that quickly gets tossed in the trash.

A reply coupon must accompany your letter. The coupon urges your people to mail back for information that was mentioned in your newsletter. Each month you can expect 2 to 3 percent of these coupons back from readers. This response opens the door to an appointment and then a sale. You can directly trace sales you would have otherwise missed to your newsletter. It's like having a sales assistant calling on your prospects and clients, setting appointments for you.

You can use each newsletter to advertise your next seminar or offer free booklets that illustrate your expertise.

Customize it with your picture, office address, and phone number. Learn how you can obtain newsletters in the appendix.

Chapter 8 Summary

Establishing yourself as an expert in senior financial services requires that you create or purchase written material—professional-quality news releases, a strong biography, questions for interviewers, your answers to those questions, newsletters, even books and booklets. All of these add up to greater credibility, both in seniors' eyes and in the eyes of media and the general public.

9 Setting Up Your Office

Seniors probably do not travel downtown very often, as most attempt to do business in their neighborhoods.

High-rise buildings are also inconvenient because it's often not obvious where to find the entrance to the underground garage, then find the elevator (which only goes to the lobby), then the other elevator that goes to the fifteenth floor, then take the right hallway to your suite.

My office is on the main street in my town. It's a two-story building with one elevator. The parking lot (no garage) is in front of the building when you drive in from the street. There is one hallway on my floor. I have made finding me as simple as possible because I am sensitive to my prospects. If you work for a financial services firm, your office location is not within your control.

It's unfortunate, but I have found that large securities firms and insurance companies typically have located their offices on the fifteenth floor of a forty-story building downtown. This location is neither convenient nor inviting for the senior prospect. If you have control over your office location, follow these guidelines.

Location Criteria

- Select a location in the neighborhood where your prospects live (not downtown).
- If your office is not on the first floor, make sure there's an elevator.
- Ensure plenty of easy-to-find parking.

Many advisors ask me if they even need an office, or if they can they work from home. In fact, I do know many successful advisors who work from home. The LTC agent you read about earlier in this book sells more than four hundred policies annually working from her home, and has all of her appointments in the prospects' homes. I also know a fee-based money manager who manages $62 million from his home. Having an office versus working from home is an individual choice. Personally, I do not enjoy going to people's homes and do not have the time. But some advisors feel that prospects are more at ease in their own homes. You certainly will get no resistance from most prospects about meeting in their homes, and you will be able to make more appointments. Often, when you follow up on a direct response lead, the prospects will resist coming to your office but will more easily agree to you coming to them.

If you do need an office occasionally, there are firms that rent offices by the hour or day very reasonably. Look under *Offices* in your yellow pages.

Office Arrangement

If possible, never speak to prospects or clients across your desk. If you have a conference table, use it. If your office can accommodate a round table, use it. Sitting with the prospect at a ninety-degree angle at a round table is far more effective at promoting a relationship than when you take the position of the cold indifferent professional from the other side of your desk.

Have your assistant offer prospects a soft drink or coffee when they enter, and make sure your reception area is neat and welcoming. First impressions are critical.

Hire an Assistant

I still meet professionals who are operating without a full-time assistant. That's simply insane. In most parts of the country, you can get a competent assistant for $35,000 annually. If that's all you want to earn, then just keep operating without an assistant and keep doing assistant's work. You'll never earn what you're really worth.

But the real value of having an assistant is not just the time it frees up for you to do the important things (like finding new clients, taking existing clients to lunch, calling existing clients, and asking for referrals). Having an assistant will free up your mind. I'm convinced that the more tasks you juggle and the more items on your mental to-do list, the less room there will be for creative ideas with high leverage.

Remember the last time you went on vacation? Or the last time you had an extended plane flight? Or any time when you were away from the distractions of the office? Did you get any great ideas? I always get my best ideas when I'm not focused on doing the next thing. If you do not have an assistant, your existence is always about doing the next thing. You not only lose the time you need to do important things, you lose the important time to even think about what the important things should be. Without an assistant, your efforts are spent on being efficient (doing things right) rather than being effective (doing the right things).

So why do so many professionals in financial services still try to get by without an assistant, or with a part-time assistant rather than full-time help? I assert that the answer is not about money. It's about fear. Professionals delay getting help because they wouldn't know what to do with the free time other than service customers, chase dividend checks, type letters, and perform other office duties. They would suddenly be faced with the fearful situation of having free time and not knowing how to use it productively.

So let me give you some ideas. Hire an assistant and use your time for these high-leverage activities:

Every Wednesday, take the names of one or two CPAs from the local phone book. Call and introduce yourself. Tell them that you have clients looking for a quality CPA who can assist with tax matters. Invite them to lunch the following week so that you can meet and see if your clients might be suitable for the CPA. At the end of the year, you will have met fifty CPAs. Send these people notes after meeting and immediately put them on your monthly newsletter list. You will generate substantial referrals from this.

You can do the same with estate planning attorneys.

Do you call every client every ninety days? If not, you're missing business and you're missing referrals.

Have you asked every client what clubs, organizations, and churches they belong to so that you can contact the program chairperson and give a talk?

If you make some time for creative thinking, you can generate dozens of ways to increase your practice. But first, you'll need to hire an assistant.

Your Appearance

During IBM's high growth years, it was nicknamed "Big Blue" because of the blue shirts its salespeople wore. Why did they wear blue shirts? Because their customers wore blue shirts, and they realized that their clients would be most comfortable with people who looked like them.

When working with seniors, do not be flashy in your dress. Men should wear dark suits and light shirts. Right now, dark shirts are fashionable, but do you know who wore dark shirts when your senior prospects were young? Gangsters. So you can be fashionable and look like a gangster (to your prospects), or you can wear light shirts and dress like your prospects do and have more business.

Women should wear dresses and skirts. No facial hair for men. You want the clean-cut, conservative look if you want to obtain the maximum number of new senior clients.

Technology: Use It in Your Business or Get Crushed

I once had a colleague ask me how I sold so much. I explained that I did not sell any more than he did; I just sold faster.

If you can sell faster, you can increase your income tremendously. Instead of making one hundred sales in a year, you can make two hundred. If you make $100,000 annually, the other advisor making $200,000 is simply selling twice as fast as you in the same 365 days.

Appropriate use of inexpensive technology can easily add five hours of sales and prospecting time to your week. That's twenty hours per month—enough to make an additional two annuity sales and generate another $4,000 to $12,000 in commissions. To use technology to sell faster, read on.

First, ever try to save money when using technology? For example, are you sharing a fax line with your phone? This does not work and never has. I promise that you are missing phone calls when your fax answers by mistake, and there have been times when people have tried to fax you and could not because your phone answered. Stop saving a measly $13 a month and install a dedicated fax line. If you don't, you are wasting time trying to get the information you should have gotten in the first place, and you may be missing valuable information or calls altogether.

By the way, regarding saving money, that's a foolish goal in the financial services business. No single financial advisor has even 1 percent of the market in your town. Delivery of financial services is highly fragmented and, therefore, it's easy to gain market share from others. It's certainly possible to double your income in a year by using the right strategies and not wasting time. If you can increase your revenue by 100 percent, isn't it a foolish focus to try and save $200 a month by cutting corners? Rather, spend your time on increasing revenues and not on saving the crumbs of cost cutting.

Back to technology. Get a fax machine that gives you a report that your fax went through to the recipient so you can stop wasting time calling after each fax to ask, "Did you get my fax?" You can find machines for well under $200 to do this.

Free e-mail accounts are great, but not if they do not accept attachments. Lots of useful e-mail is sent with attachments. If your e-mail does not allow attachments, get a new e-mail account, even if it costs you $9.95 a month. If you do not have e-mail, that's like not having a telephone number. You have cut off much of your communication with the outside world. You are wasting time accepting and making calls and sending faxes that can be better handled by sending and receiving e-mails.

E-mail allows you to reduce the use of the telephone, thus saving enormous time. The telephone is an extremely inefficient device. Remember, it was invented in the 1860s. If you're still relying on an invention from the last century to power your business, look out. Your competitors will crush you.

TWO REASONS THE TELEPHONE IS INEFFICIENT

1. Look at how much time you waste playing telephone tag. Most times, you really do not need to talk to the other person; you could send an e-mail with attached documents and fulfill the communication. Most communication is one way: You need to deliver or get information. The telephone is a two-way device and should be used only when you need to have a discussion or make contact to maintain a relationship. Analyze your phone conversations today and see how many (I'll bet 90 percent) are one-way communications, which do not require the inefficient use of the telephone.
2. The telephone often gets you into time-wasting, non-essential discussions. You end up wasting twelve minutes chatting, when that time could have been used making two sales calls.

Make heavy use of the Internet. (You can get free Internet access and e-mail from many sources, or for $10 a month if you do not want to see any ads.) Customers and prospects like to see items that have been published because published documents have credibility. Published documents include items from the newspaper, magazines, and the Internet. (Please note that product brochures and sales pieces have no credibility, and that's why your prospects never read them.) You can find almost any information on the Internet in a few minutes, print, and send and/or e-mail to your prospect to support your point. This information will have credibility with your prospect.

Regarding Internet searches, realize that no single search engine indexes more than 15 percent of the pages on the Internet. Therefore, you want to use a tool that searches multiple search engines simultaneously. Many Internet users use Dogpile (*www.dogpile.com*). I prefer Copernic (*www.copernic.com*), which is software that runs on your own computer and performs a search on ten search engines at once and provides a single output list. The software is free.

Do not waste time waiting for Internet pages to download or for your computer to log on. Get a DSL line or cable connection, which is always on (no need to dial up to the Internet), and your pages will load in lightning speed. It's a really foolish waste of time waiting for Internet pages to load over your 56k modem. Our DSL line is $39 per month and allows everyone in our office to use the Internet at four times the speed of a 56k modem. It's always on.

I am amazed when I call financial professionals and get a busy signal. That should never happen. Do you want to lose business? For about $8 a month, the phone company will give you a voice-mail box so that even if twenty people call you at once, they will get your voice-mail system and can leave a message. Make sure no one ever gets a busy signal. If you have your own voice-mail system, make sure that you have more lines coming in to your office than there are employees. Otherwise, when everyone is on the phone, the next incoming caller will get a busy signal. It will cost about $13 per month to add a line.

Subscribe to publications like *Value Line* (stock information) and *Morningstar* (mutual fund information) on CD-ROM. Together, they will cost you less than $1,100 per year. They provide you the information necessary to show a new prospect how their stocks and funds have been performing and which items should be sold (and invested with you). Without this convincing third-party evidence, is it any wonder that some prospects are not just accepting your word for it? There is nothing more powerful to convince a prospect than printed third-party evidence. I used these tools to free up millions of dollars annually to place under fee-based money management.

Monthly Costs of Solutions Covered in This Chapter

Separate fax phone line	$17
E-mail and Internet access	Included with DSL Line
DSL line	$49
Additional phone line to eliminate busy signals	$39
Voice mail to eliminate busy signals	$8
Subscriptions, *Value Line* and *Morningstar*	$91
TOTAL	**$204**

Have you been saving this $204 a month while your efficient competitors are grabbing the sales that could have been yours?

What to Do Monday Morning— And Every Day Thereafter!

Get your wardrobe in shape and your office in shape. If you need to have a different location, then call a real estate broker to find you one. Get serious. Jump in the pool rather than stick your toe in.

Most important, based on the principles in this book about senior psychology and sales methods, develop or purchase (see appendix) marketing programs that will *have seniors coming to you:*

- a seminar program that you will do monthly,
- an advertising program offering a valuable educational booklet, and
- a direct mail program that has seniors responding for a free quote or service.

I have spoken with many advisors who tell me that a particular marketing program worked well, but they stopped using it. As crazy as this sounds, I hear it often. Applying marketing programs is no different from going to the gym. If you go for two months and then quit, I promise you your waistline won't look any different two months later. Marketing, as with exercise, requires a consistent application to pay off.

Do not give up after thirty days. Every successful system is developed over time by testing different copy, using different magazines and publications, changing seminar times and titles, etc. Use the parts of the program that work for you and just change the components that need to be improved.

For example, we had a planner using our seminar system and getting good attendance. But he did not get sufficient numbers of attendees to schedule an appointment. So we worked with him to stick to the script for getting appointments. We isolated the problem area and then just worked on that. Tenacity pays. Consistency is essential.

I have met too many advisors making a half-hearted attempt and waiting until the big payoff to move to a better office, to get an assistant, to get better clothes. *Get serious from the start.* Here's the secret: You need to invest first and jump in to get the big payoff. As one mentor of mine said, "You need to put wood in the fireplace before it gives off any heat."

Book Summary

You now have the strategic and tactical components of a financial services practice that can assist thousand of seniors, as well as earn you a handsome living. To get started, schedule a seminar, get appointments scheduled, and then keep up the momentum.

Best of luck to you. Please consider us a resource to help you build a quality business as thousands of other financial professionals have. We have outlined a number of tools in the appendix that can help speed your success.

About the Author

Larry Klein, CPA/PFS, MBA, CSA

Larry Klein, President of NF Communications, Inc. has assisted thousands of financial service professionals to increase their clients and income. Over 10,000 financial professionals use his marketing systems to attract more and better clients. Mr. Klein started his career as a CPA with a "big eight" accounting firm and moved into advising retail clients as a Vice President of Investments at Great Western Financial Securities, and then as a First Vice President and branch manager with Prudential Securities (where he was in the top 5% of producers).

In 1987, the leading magazine for the brokerage industry, *Registered Representative,* selected Larry as one of the Ten Outstanding Investment Brokers in the United States. Mr. Klein is a Certified Senior Advisor (one of 8000 in the United States), a Registered Investment Advisor, and he holds an MBA from Harvard Business School.

Larry has lectured widely on financial topics at Boston University, University of San Francisco, and University of California at Berkeley. He has written dozens of articles on financial topics spanning estate planning, retirement plans and social security.

He has been interviewed in industry publications including *On Wall Street, Registered Representative Magazine, Research Magazine, Advisor Today, The Agent Sales Journal, Life Insurance Selling, National Underwriter* and *Financial Advisor Pro.* In these industry publications he counsels financial services professionals how to use smart and efficient seminars, direct mail and direct response marketing to obtain substantial increases in their income.

He is the author of Marketing Financial Services to Seniors, *Retirement Investing, Asset Protection and Wealth Preservation,* and *Mistakes Retirees Make With Their Finances.*

APPENDIX

Programs to Make You a Big Producer in the Senior Market

AND

Systems to Increase Your Commissions and Fees

FOR FINANCIAL PLANNERS, LIFE AGENTS, STOCKBROKERS, INVESTMENT ADVISORS, AND CPAS

- Sell More Annuities
- Pack Your Seminar Room Every Time
- Have Your Own Financial Book—Be an Author
- Get Interviewed in Your Local Newspaper
- Make a Fortune from Fee-Based Money Management
- Generate Appointments with a Client/Prospect Newsletter
- Open More Investment Accounts with Mechanical Money Management
- Sell LTC with Seminars
- Be an Advanced IRA Distribution Expert
- Senior Leads Program

AVAILABLE FROM NF COMMUNICATIONS, INC.

(800) 980-0192 OPTION 4

WWW.NFCOM.COM

FOR ADDITIONAL DETAILS AND PRICES, VISIT WWW.NFCOM.COM/BOOK.HTM, OR CALL (800) 980-0192 OPTION 4.

If You Want to Increase Your Business . . .

This appendix provides brief descriptions of the 10,000 marketing systems in use by over ten thousand producers who significantly increase their business in the senior market. These systems were developed and tested in an actual financial-planning practice and are continually refined for even greater results. We are so sure of their results that the seminar systems and the direct marketing system come with a ninety-day guarantee (conditions apply, call for details).

It's insane to waste your time developing and testing systems when others have already done the work. The big producers in our business just use already developed systems that work so they can spend more time with qualified prospects. And these systems will show you several ways to fill your day talking to qualified prospects.

If you would like complete details after reading these brief descriptions, please fax the order form at the back of this book, or download the details *immediately* from our web site:

www.nfcom.com/book

"Over the last four years, I have spent a fortune on sales systems that promised to double my production. Unfortunately, many of these programs failed to deliver what they claimed. By far, your marketing programs are a standout among a very crowded field."

C. BINSTOCK, DULUTH, MN

"If you are in the financial services business and want to focus on the senior market, get everything Larry has to offer and keep pushing him to come up with more. They are the best resources in the country if this is your market."

H. KAPLAN, TENAFLY, NJ

FOR ADDITIONAL DETAILS AND PRICES, VISIT WWW.NFCOM.COM/BOOK.HTM, OR CALL (800) 980-0192 OPTION 4.

"The annuity program is by far the best lead source I have ever used. I have in my database over 250 very qualified leads since I started using the annuity system. By the way, did I mention I have produced over $800,000 in annuity premiums using your system? It works!"

D. RAY, CHARLOTTE, NC

"I have used many marketing programs over the last six years and have found none that comes close to your annuity sales system. Your approach, as simple as it may sound, has worked wonders for my business. Thanks."

C. MEEKS, BALTIMORE, MD

"This package is easily worth its weight in gold, and we highly recommend it (of course, only if you're not in our area). We've been told by attendees many times that this is 'the greatest seminar that we've ever been to.' You saved us years of learning by trial and error."

C. NICHOLS & C. SCOTT, FULLERTON, CA

"I just wanted to let you know how our last seminar went. It seemed like people were coming out of the woodwork. They just kept coming in! We had to scramble to get chairs and had to send someone to Kinko's to make more packets. I had to practically scream to be heard across this huge, packed room. It was truly amazing."

C. BUTLER, OVERLAND PARK, KS

"This has been the single most important thing I have done this year to encourage high-quality referrals—and it has worked! I have raised over $3 million in managed money accounts from referrals [in about five months] and I directly relate this to the Retirement Investing program."

N. FRANKLE, WOODLAND HILLS, CA

Marketing Systems to Attract and Serve Affluent Seniors

SEMINAR SYSTEM

While some advisors may think "seminars don't work" or "my area is over-seminared," we've been using the same winning formula to fill seminar rooms without serving meals for 18 years. Our system shows you how to pack the room with a compelling invitation, make a presentation that motivates and provides you the system to set appointments with **at least** 50% of attendees before they leave the seminar. We even prepare the invitation mailing for you. It's turnkey, it's easy, it's inexpensive and it's profitable. And for the attendees who don't set an appointment right away, we give you a six-month subscription to the best senior newsletter that has prospects call you.

Seminar System with Weekly Coaching
Call for current pricing
90 Day Guarantee (see www.nfcom.com/show/guarantee)
Most modules NASD Reviewed

FOR ADDITIONAL DETAILS AND PRICES, VISIT WWW.NFCOM.COM/BOOK.HTM, OR CALL (800) 980-0192 OPTION 4.

Available Seminar Modules:

SIX MISTAKES RETIREES MAKE WITH THEIR FINANCES

For the comprehensive financial planner seeking to gather all of the client's assets for investments and insurance. **Topics covered:** Life Expectancy, How the Stock Market Really Works, Mistakes With Mutual Funds, LTC, Annuities, Fixed Income Investing.

RETIREMENT SURVIVAL

For the insurance oriented advisor seeking to gather all of the client's assets for investments and insurance **Topics covered:** IRA Distributions, Three Ways to Avoid Capital Gains Tax, Overpaying Tax on Your Mutual Funds, Investing in Stocks, Funding Education, Estate Planning.

ANNUITY SEMINAR

For the insurance advisor seeking to maximize sales of annuities.

IRA DISTRIBUTION PLANNING

For the advisor seeking to attract the 4,000 people a day that turn age 70 ½ and must starting taking IRA distributions and have no clue about the complex decisions they need to make.

Income Tax Reduction and Estate Tax Elimination

Of the 6 topics covered, 5 have nothing to do with saving the kids estate taxes and the success of this seminar is not dependent on estate tax rates. For advisors seeking people with at least $1.5 million of investment assets. **Topics covered:** Create Wealth Outside Your Estate, Shift Wealth Outside Your Estate, Gift Wealth and Spend It Too, Discount It, Leverage It, Freeze It.

Asset Protection Seminar/LTC

For insurance producers who seek to maximize LTC sales

Seminar System with Weekly Coaching
Call for current pricing
90 Day Guarantee (see www.nfcom.com/show/guarantee)
Most modules NASD Reviewed

DIRECT MARKETING SYSTEM

Direct mail and advertising pay like slot machines when you know how to use them. But most advisors use ads and mail developed to appeal to the "left brain"—the logical side of the brain. But people buy emotionally—their decision to act is centered in the right brain and our ads and direct mail prices speak to their center of motivation. These ads and mail pieces offer a booklet that we personalize with your name, credentials, photo, biography and contact information, Upon receipt, the senior immediately sees that you are a professional, a consultant-not merely another financial sales person.

Our system shows you every step:

- Where to run the most effective and least expensive ads
- How to find the best lists of buyers for the direct mail
- The script to follow up on every call and have as many as 50% set appointments

Originally developed as a way to help advisors generate some extra income in as little as 15 hours a month, some advisors have dumped all other marketing activities and use our direct marketing system to generate all of their income.

Available Direct Marketing Modules:

IRA Distribution

Attracts people nearing age 70½ with six and seven figure IRA needing help with distribution issues.

Long-Term Care

Attracts seniors who have been thinking about long term care insurance.

Existing Annuity Owners

Attracts people with large annuities to exchange or convert to life policies.

CD Shoppers

Attracts seniors seeking higher interest, often prospects for a wide range of fixed income offerings.

Every Direct Marketing Module includes:

- 100 personalized booklets
- The tested and proven advertisement
- Follow up letters
- The winning telephone script
- Six months of a "drip" senior newsletter for people who won't meet right away

Direct Marketing System with Weekly Coaching
Call for current pricing
90 Day Guarantee (see www.nfcom.com/pdf/guarantee.pdf)
Most modules NASD Reviewed

Never Prospect Strangers Again!
Client Referral System

We have a proven system that really works and has been tested and re-tested. You can easily turn 100 clients into 500 clients or more in two years. A lot of referral systems are based on the personality of the advisor. But this system works for anybody. We've tossed out all the wrong things you've been taught about referrals and show you the three elements if getting referrals to end all other prospecting. **You learn:**

- How to get an introduction to each referral
- How to warm up the referral before you contact them
- How to build on each referral for additional introductions

Here's what one recent system owner said:

"Just thought I'd let you know, I recently ordered your Client Referral System. I followed your instructions to the letter, watched the video and called two clients to test the process out. I am happy to say the system worked like a charm. In a low-key, easy fashion I now have 50 introductions. I guess I will be very busy in December! This system is unbelievable—simple and effective." J. Keeter, Anaheim, CA

You get the complete workbook plus a video showing you exactly what to do and say each step of the way. Just follow the simple, non-threatening, non-embarrassing steps and you'll never have to prospect strangers again!

FOR ADDITIONAL DETAILS AND PRICES, VISIT WWW.NFCOM.COM/BOOK.HTM, OR CALL (800) 980-0192 OPTION 4.

How to Conduct a Prospect Interview & Close More Sales

Most advisors cannot sell and they don't even know it. They think that selling is talking at the client to explain features ands benefits. Find out how Larry Klein became a million-dollar producer with his definition of selling, "The asking of appropriate questions so that the prospect sees the solutions for themselves." You'll see how a master does it on video and the entire process is explained. You learn how to "unsell" the prospect's current investments—a step that many advisors miss and then lose the opportunity for new clients. Get ready to have most of what you believe about selling destroyed—and learn how to triple your income with a new way to present.

Call for current pricing (step discount available when purchased with a seminar system or direct marketing system).

How to Double Your Income As a Fee-Based Money Manager

Want to capture the trend of fee-based management? Not sure how to transition your clients? Not sure how to work with new prospects on a fee basis? Feel like you don't know enough about investments? We teach you everything you need to know to create a mountain of residual fee income. No more starting from zero on January 1st. Wealthy clients want fee-based relationships and they are concerned about potential conflict of interests in commission relationships. We also teach you how to cultivate these affluent relationships and manage investment portfolios better than 83% of the portfolio managers (and we've got the data to prove it).

Go with the market trend to fee-based management before your commission business disappears.

This deluxe package includes 1) your choice of any one of our seminar systems, 2) Money Management System, 3) six months of the Direct Response Newsletter and 4) Personal Coaching.

FOR ADDITIONAL DETAILS AND PRICES, VISIT WWW.NFCOM.COM/BOOK.HTM, OR CALL (800) 980-0192 OPTION 4.

Mechanical Money-Management System

Would you like to raise a lot more money for money management? It's easy when you show prospects how they and their advisor mess up their own portfolios. They have no system and are constantly shooting from the hip after watching CNBC or reading Money magazine. Worse, even their brokers have no strategies for them to follow.

Americans and their advisors invest based on whim and fleeting opinion. When you show prospects how you use a mechanical system to invest, they will see that you have a discipline and you are the professional they should trust. And you'll have a lot more time when you have all of your client portfolios on a mechanical system that needs to be rebalanced only once annually. You learn how to present these systems at a seminar and one-on-one and have prospects open new accounts with you.

We show you how to present the Dow Dividend Strategy, the Value Line Strategy, and other mechanical systems and how to use these systems to turn your practice into a well-oiled machine.

If you like the idea of commissions (or fees) every year, retaining clients, and doing little work, then this system is for you. It's the fastest, easiest way to manage clients' money and deliver great performance without watching the stock market. This is also a great way for those who have little stock market experience (life agents or series 6 licensees) to start managing clients' money with great results.

FOR ADDITIONAL DETAILS AND PRICES, VISIT WWW.NFCOM.COM/BOOK.HTM, OR CALL (800) 980-0192 OPTION 4.

Senior Leads

If you would like 2-3 emails a day from motivated seniors, the senior leads program is for you. From over 100 ads that we run every day on the Internet, seniors request booklets on various topics (see booklets described on page 171). When you register to receive these requests from seniors in your zip codes, the requests appear in your email within 5 minutes. We show you how to follow up and set appointments. Now, you have a way to use the Internet to make money and gain clients.

After a nominal registration fee, leads are $10 each and you can stop the service at any time. **Complete details at www.nfcom.com/seniorleads**

Senior Web Sites

Get the only senior-oriented web site available from our marketing partner, Financial Visions. If you're an independent advisor and not with a big name firm, you have a credibility problem with seniors. The fastest way to convince them of your stature is to have every prospect visit your web site before you meet. When they see 100+ senior articles, calculators for solving financial problems, information and links to senior-specific issues, and professionally-designed graphics, they'll think you employ 50 people!

For about $1 a day, you can make a superior impression and look like one of the big boys.

Download a free copy of "Ten Ways to Profit with a Web Site" at **www.fvisions.com**

Have Your Own TV Show

You may not be as funny as Leno or Letterman, but you can have your own TV show. We show you how to produce and air 6 shows for under $2000. Scripts are NASD reviewed and you get the step by step process of how to use the Community Access TV station in your area and how to have your clients, prospects and other seniors tune in. We show you the mechanism to convert viewers to clients. Other advisors have radio and TV shows, why not you? What better way to show prospects that you are different than every other advisor in town.

Public Relations Kit

Would you like to get your name in the local newspaper four to six times per year? Or have your articles published? You can with NF Communications' public relations kit. We'll show you how we get interviewed by reporters repeatedly and have a stack of articles. If you'd like to become well known in your town, this inexpensive system is for you.

Direct-Response Newsletter

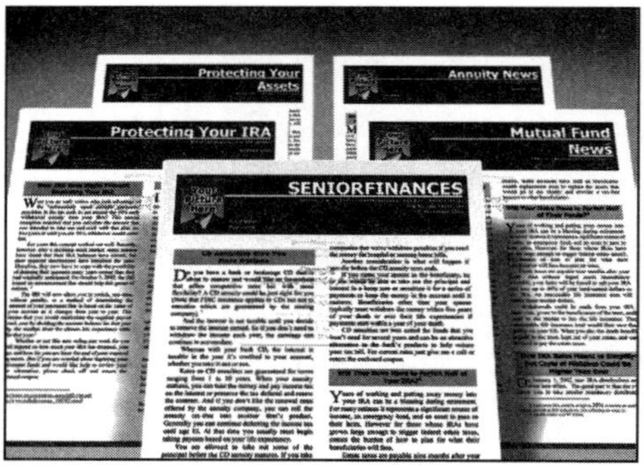

Each month, send a newsletter to clients and prospects, and each month get ten to twenty replies asking for more information. That's right—ten to twenty people ask you for more information or appointments about investment or insurance opportunities. Finally have a newsletter that pays for itself with measurable results. Use a newsletter that helps you make more sales and that directly generates profits.

Most importantly, this newsletter helps you convert those prospects who come to your seminars or meet you, but never take action. When they keep getting your newsletter, they never forget you. When they're ready, you're the one they call because you're the one who's been there. It's the best return you'll ever have for such a low cost per prospect.

Once you subscribe, you can download any of 6 newsletters we publish for you each month. You can choose from these senior specific newsletters:

- General Senior Newsletter
- IRA
- Fixed Annuities
- Retirement Income Sources
- Mutual Funds and Variable Annuities
- Long Term Care

Each Article is NASD Reviewed

FOR ADDITIONAL DETAILS AND PRICES, VISIT WWW.NFCOM.COM/BOOK.HTM, OR CALL (800) 980-0192 OPTION 4.

Personalized Booklets for Instant Credibility

The quickest way to indicate your expertise is with your wisdom in writing. But writing can be very time consuming. So NF Communications offers booklets that you can send to prospects and clients, booklets that are personalized with your name, picture, biography, contact information and even your logo on the cover!

AVAILABLE TITLES:

Annuity Owner Opportunities (16 pages)—a motivating booklet that shows existing annuity owners the mistakes they make and the knowledge they lack, and why they need to call you.

Avoid Mistakes in Buying Long-Term Care Insurance (15 pages)—show your prospects that you're not just another long term care salesperson—you'll actually show them how to avoid mistakes in making this important purchase—and they'll choose you.

Money Management (14 pages)—A booklet which shows stock investors why a mechanical system is better than what they do on their own AND what most professional money managers do—they shoot from the hip. They'll see you have a better system.

FOR ADDITIONAL DETAILS AND PRICES, VISIT WWW.NFCOM.COM/BOOK.HTM, OR CALL (800) 980-0192 OPTION 4.

Mistakes in Selecting Mutual Funds (15 pages)—shows investors what they don't know (but think they do) about investing in funds and they will need your advice.

IRA Distribution Mistakes and How to Avoid Them (17 pages)—This booklet is designed to accompany our Advanced IRA Distribution Seminar System and can be used by any planner interested in this area to show affluent seniors your expertise.

Seven Ways Retirees Can Cut Taxes (15 pages)—This booklet highlights the tax saving virtues of annuities and VUL.

CD Shoppers' Guide (12pages)—This booklet shows seniors how to get higher interest and generates calls for all types of fixed income investments and fixed annuities.

Have Your Own Financial Book

Would you like to have the credibility of an author? You can! We will write your book for you. Our professional writers turn your ideas into your own unique, published masterpiece. Or here are three easy-to-read, generic books on financial topics of interest to seniors, already composed. We can print the books with your name, picture, and biography. How do you think prospects react when you hand them a copy of your book? We show you ten ways to use your book to quickly gain more clients.

This is the easiest way to build your credibility and differentiate yourself from every other broker, planner, and advisor in town.

Call (800) 980-0192 option 4 for pricing, information on protected territories or to receive a free sample of a book.

NASD Reviewed

FOR ADDITIONAL DETAILS AND PRICES, VISIT WWW.NFCOM.COM/BOOK.HTM, OR CALL (800) 980-0192 OPTION 4.

How To Become A Million Dollar Producer

Larry Klein has worked with thousands of advisors and has isolated 6 activities that the large producers have in common. Adopt even one of these activities and watch your income increase by 30%. This is a must read for any advisor who wants to get on the fast track and understand right now what seven figure producers do to stand out from the crowd—$19.95

Financial Jokes

Get your point across better with humor. Here's the book for you: 400 Greatest Jokes for Financial Professionals. When you add humor, you close more appointments from seminars and more sales from presentations.

This book has jokes, stories, and poems about the stock market, investing, health care, CPAs, attorneys, bankers, stockbrokers, technology, money, marriage, estate planning, insurance, and patience. Afraid that you can't deliver a joke well? Don't worry, an audio CD is included that teaches you how to employ the four most important aspects to tell great jokes.

Lighten up your presentations with a little humor and watch your sales take off!

Joke Book plus Audio on How to Deliver a Great Joke—$39.95

FOR ADDITIONAL DETAILS AND PRICES, VISIT
WWW.NFCOM.COM/BOOK.HTM,
OR CALL (800) 980-0192 OPTION 4.

Have Larry Klein as Your Next Speaker

Larry Klein passed the CPA exam and graduated from college at age 19 and earned his Harvard MBA at age 24. For the past 18 years, Larry has used his acumen to serve individual investors and in 1997, turned his attention to help advisors rapidly grow their businesses to serve their clients.

MDRT, NAIFA, Society of Certified Senior Advisors, Charles Schwab and State Farm are just a few of the institutions that have featured Larry as a speaker. There is no one in the US as qualified to speak on marketing financial services and no one who knows the growing senior market more intimately. His articles and interviews have appeared in every trade publication including Advisor Today, Research Magazine, Financial Planning, National Underwriter and On Wall Street. Over a dozen broker dealers include his articles in their advisor newsletters. See speaking topics and feedback letters at:

www.nfcom.com/show/institutions/lkspeaking

About NF Communications, Inc.

On his way to the $1 million production level at Prudential Securities, Larry Klein tried his hand at managing the branch. He implemented the marketing systems he used in his own business for the other brokers, and in six months the branch went from a ranking of thirty-one in its region to the number two spot.

Out of this success in helping others increase their business, Larry started NF Communications to design, test, and distribute highly effective marketing systems for stockbrokers, financial planners, life insurance agents, and investment advisors. All of these systems are designed for prospecting where the money is: in the senior market, investors age sixty-plus.

These previously described programs have been thoroughly tested and proven in Larry's practice or the practices of other financial advisors. We are so confident of their success, based on the ten thousand systems now in use across the United States, that the seminar program and direct marketing program come with a ninety-day guarantee (conditions apply—call for details).

Many of the programs have been NASD reviewed and already approved for use by major wire houses and insurance companies.

Call with questions, for current prices, or to order:

(800) 980-0192 option 4

Visit us on the web:

www.nfcom.com/book.htm

NF COMMUNICATIONS, INC.

1700 NORTH BROADWAY, SUITE 405